The Parkestone Foundation Inc.
Proceeds from the sale of this book go to the Parkestone Foundation Inc.

The Parkestone Foundation was initially constituted as an Association in 1982 following a generous bequest by an Adelaide gay man, Peter Nation, which enabled the establishment of a trust fund. The foundation is managed by a committee of honorary trustees who ensure that the trust fund is used for its intended purpose which is to support LGBTIQA+ community projects consistent with its objectives. Since its inception, the foundation has allocated over $40,000 to support community projects in South Australia.

Additional donations and further information about the Parkestone Foundation Inc.'s work can be found at www.parkestonetrust.org

Peering Through

Published by the Buon-Cattivi Press, 2018
Adelaide, Australia
ISBN (PAPERBACK) 978-0-9953661-8-3
ISBN (EBOOK) 978-0-9953661-7-6

Book design and cover illustration
by Andrew Crooks

Peering Through

Sharing Decades of Queer Experiences

Edited by Dr Alex Dunkin and Greg Fell

Buon-Cattivi Press
Adelaide, Australia

Foreword

Australia's queer history is a complex one. Over the decades identities within the queer community have risen and fallen. Their history can be traced along with the major social and cultural events occurring at the time. Several internationally recognised moments, such as the South Australian decriminalisation of homosexuality, marked major changes in the lives of the LGBTIQ community.

In other cases, such large changes in the legal rights of the LGBTIQ community passed over some who identify as part of the community as they continued to strive for the best in theirs and their family lives. The level of interaction with different moments in Australia's queer history provides an interesting tapestry to be collated.

There are lifetimes of experiences hidden out there in the LGBTIQ world. In particular, the elders of the community have held a wealth of knowledge based upon their time growing and thriving in a world designed to attack and sometimes persecute them just for being who they are. Each experience is unique, layered in individual complexities that arrive from living a full life.

Unfortunately the passing of time and the inevitable

are causing some of these experiences to fade, in some cases leaving our world when the elder does. *Peering Through* is just one small step that is seeking to prevent the invaluable lessons from our community from being lost. The stories collected are a beautiful variety of life goals achieved, struggles overcome, and loses recognised. Through this project the stories are released into the world where a new set of voices can be added to the permanent records.

Peering Through

Sharing Decades of Queer Experiences

Contents

1899	1
1940s	2
1950s	14
1960s	31
1970s	43
1980s	94
1990s	130
2000s	146
2010s	184
Post	204
Endnotes	210

Index by Name

David D	15, 40, 69, 77, 114, 140, 186
David H	4, 63, 76, 88, 164, 187, 200
Gabby	24, 80, 107, 132, 142, 153, 159, 190
Hugh	3, 26, 35, 55, 66, 100, 189
Mahamati	8, 48, 83, 108, 120, 167, 196
Michael	4, 21, 41, 58, 68, 96, 177
Philip	33, 57, 91, 104, 156
Thomas	19, 60, 149, 179
Travis	50, 73, 98, 137, 197

Disclaimer
Some names have been changed.

1899

The Beginning of Australian Anti-LGBTIQ Laws.
Australia's history in its negative attitude toward LGBTIQ people extends over a hundred years. Like many colonies that preceded it, the country inherited British laws that parliament may later alter or repeal.[1] One such alteration to laws include the penalty for sodomy conviction reduced from execution to life in prison, via Queensland's Criminal Code Act 1899 that came into force 1st January 1901.[2] However, the term hangover is apt here, as this change occurred decades after Britain itself had removed the death penalty for sodomy. The Act was passed by the Queensland Government prior to federation, and so it was not binding upon all Australian colonies (later states and territories), which did not move to the lesser penalty.[3]

Sex between consenting male adults continued to be crimes in some Australian states up until 1997. Female same-sex sex acts were never illegal under British or Australian law, often because people publicly denied that it ever happened.

1940s

Post War Times

The great wars created major disturbances on Australian social, cultural, and political situations. Families were torn apart, laws focussed on the war efforts and the repercussions were felt across the nation. Many LGBTIQ service men and women served in silence and even upon their return to Australia they were not welcomed to be open in the Returned Service League. During their service romantic liaisons did occur and as one serviceman stated 'we might as well be happy while we've the chance'.[4]

The history of the Peering Through Queer Elders begins during and after this period.

Hugh

There are two strands to my story. One about guilt, agonising and desperate soul-destroying guilt, eventually leading to self-acceptance. The other is the light on the hill (which for me was the 1975 decriminalisation of homosexuality in South Australia).

I was born in 1936 and grew up in Sydney. Sydney for other people is the land of the Mardi Gras and gay permissiveness. For me it was the land of aunts. Everywhere I turned I'd always see an aunt, and so it was extremely respectable and very restrictive. I was also bought up strict Presbyterian, that means no sex outside marriage and a lot of other little restrictions. Dancing was frowned on. Swearing was not on. You could drink, but only if you were a responsible adult. However, thanks to my mother's warm nature and cultured background, and the enthusiasm of my siblings, I remember an enormous amount of fun and laughter through an atmosphere that often threatened to be too strained.

I was very, very active in the church. I was in the choir—I just happened to be born with a good singing voice, I taught in the Sunday school and I led the Fellowship. In other words it was a social centre for me, very much so, and that was quite a problem, to find something to replace that later on, because when you're involved to that extent it's actually very supportive and you're very loath to let go.

Michael

I was born in 1943 and grew up in a small country town in the lower-north of SA. My parents were the first of three generations of early settlers to seek employment beyond farming. My father's family had immigrated from Silesia in 1848, my mother's from Scotland in 1854. Both sides were largely unsuccessful financially, often farming on marginal land and subject to the vagaries of the weather and rural economics.

In the aftermath of the Depression my father undertook a fitter and turner apprenticeship and remained employed in the same manufacturing firm for forty-six years. Because his employment was deemed a 'reserve occupation' during World War II, he was denied enlistment in the RAAF. My mother trained as a nurse in a country hospital.

David H

I grew up in the suburbs of Melbourne around Dandenong, which is about twenty five kilometres out of Melbourne, something like that, very suburban. I have no wish to ever go back there thank you very much. We're talking starting from 1948 when we migrated here. I was a three-year-old and my parents came from the suburbs of metropolitan London, and I remember my mother complaining that the biscuits were made out of sawdust and the transport was terrible—it was a red rattler railway carriage. I have never forgotten: in the main street of Dandenong there used to be date palms down the centre and she couldn't get over the fact (coming from London) that there was a woman who literally took horse and jig down the main street who would go to the Dandenong market on Wednesday, so that blew her mind. When you think about it, yes, it would be confronting so there we go.

I think I had the odd friend here and there. I didn't try to make it very easy to make friends. I don't do large groups very well. I'm quite good talking one-to-one and I like that. Walking into the party situation I really find difficult and I do not have the sports gene in any way shape or form and so that is also something that sets you apart and different. My one sporting achievement is being forced to play cricket in secondary school, while I remember this quite well, standing on the edges probably thinking about the book I was reading and the ball comes flying up and they all yell out to me 'drop it, drop it' and I actually caught it. That was my only achievement. I had some friends, quite often they were misfits in their own way if you want put it that way but not very many of them, just the odd one here and there.

The way I look at that is I've done an awful lot of work on myself and I see it is peeling back the layers of an onion (if you like) or the lotus opening up before you get to the jewel in the centre, it's been a lot of work. I had a very poor self-image, particularly to do with my sexuality and also just me generally, and I think it came from my family and my upbringing and I had to work on that to get where I'd got to now. It's been a big task.

I don't ever remember being told homosexuality is wrong or anything like that and part of the problem was having two parents who were both English, born in 1915, who were in their own ways repressed, and they lived through the Depression. My father was a very introverted man, my mother was much more outgoing. Their marriage—because of the differences in the personality—became hard work for both of them and I think my mother had a lot of anger because she ended up having to do everything, paying the bills, organising the schooling, all that stuff because my father was a bit of a 'Peter Pan' in his own way. He'd been bashed by the nuns, for example, for writing with his left hand and forced to use his right hand. He loathed the nuns after that. He had lost his father in the First World War when he was about one-year-old so he didn't really have the experience of being fathered, so how was he to know what to do and lucky him he had this cuckoo nest (me) who loved reading books and playing classical piano. He was a plumber basically so we couldn't meet on any level very easily at all and I remember him saying to me once 'why you want to read all them books?' Later on when I went to my mother and I said I want to study classical music, it was something along the lines of 'all those composers were crazy why would you want to do that?' and even when I actually came out to her and we had the conversation it always referred back to her. I was an extension of her (and we're talking not a small child at this point) and I remember the conversation was 'I don't think you are (gay)'. So it was like a game to her with some reality that was important to me and she would say 'oh no, that's not right' so I was never heard ticked, it was always crossed, you see what I mean.

That really didn't help and because of their era they weren't at all open about sexual things at all, no matter what the sexual thing was. So to have something as way out as being a 'poofter' was 'oh my god what happened, what did we do?'. So that was the background that I grew up in and I had to do a lot of repairing and all that stuff. My sister took a different line. She rebelled, which I did not do. I tended to internalise it all, which is much harder actually. So as I said over the years that I had to peel those layers back that I put up to protect myself because it couldn't really get through to either of them.

Well, for who influenced me, going on from what I said I think in a negative way it was my parents. I mean I love them but I can remember separating myself from my father quite distinctly when he lost his temper with me one day and I thought—I actually remember thinking—'you will never hurt me again' and I just put a wall up. I got on generally well with my mother. She had a big influence on me and she'd been very musical through her early life and gone to theatre and opera and stuff in London, and she actually got me learning piano which I obviously still play which was very important. As far as parents go, she was the one that I got on better with in a sense so I'd probably say her in a lot of ways. As I sort of came to late adolescence, early twenties I think I was just starting on my voyage and it's taken a long time and I don't really remember anyone being there in a mentoring sense.

Mahamati

My story is probably a little bit different to the ordinary. My father was totally blind and had been blind since a small child. He had meningitis, so I grew up with a father that was different. He was quite remarkable as I look back on it. He worked at a sheltered workshop that the Royal Institute for the Blind did making mattings. He was also a musician and he played in lots of bands, dance bands and orchestras, which is how he met my mother in a small town—Rendelsham in South Australia. During the war years teams of blind musicians used to go out and entertain the country people and they'd be billeted at different people's homes and that's how he met my mother. She lived a fairly isolated life in a small, small town in the South East of South Australia and she only went to school until grade seven and I'm not sure what she did in those years before she met my father. I guess it seemed quite exciting to her. They did a lot of touring around and travelling around South Australia and Victoria and when they got married she used to travel with the band, with the orchestras at different times.

They eventually settled in Prospect. My grandfather also lived with us, after my grandmother died. With him from Rendelsham he brought about six to eight kangaroos he used to tame and breed, for what purpose I don't know but he used to do these corny picture postcards of kangaroos playing cricket and send them all over the world. Anyway, some of the kangaroos got shipped off to the zoo but others lived with us and that was another different thing in the neighbourhood.

But, probably the biggest part of my childhood was that I had polio. I was one of the first kids infected in the epidemic of 1948-9, so I spent a lot of my childhood in hospital and in rehabilitation. I was infected when I was three and I didn't get home until I was seven and a half so it was quite a lot of childhood away from home and in those days institutions were fairly daunting, parents visited less.

So I came home and I was still on this frame which is sort of this big thing that sits you in the living room and I did correspondence lessons for grade one and two, my mother taught me. I didn't actually go to school until I was probably in grade three. This was all happening in suburban Prospect, which was interesting in lots of ways. I have written a fair bit about it at different times in my life and because my father had gone to school at what's called Townsend House here, which was an institution for blind and deaf and mute kids (or deaf and dumb as they called it then, terrible name). So that was his really strong cohort of friendships that he'd been to boarding school with every other week and he'd be home on the weekend. They would all visit and in that time I guess I learned a lot. My dad being blind he could sign, he could sign to his deaf friends, they could see what he signed but for them to converse back to him those who didn't have much voice or speaking would have to sign into his hand and that was a fairly slow and cumbersome job and seeing as I was sort of just on my frame doing nothing at home between school lessons he taught me how to sign so that I could then be the interpreter. So, he could sign away, they could see it, they could sign back and I could speak it for them. I guess I learned all the swear words and lots about the Cheltenham races, Brunswick and what horses are good.

My education was a little bit different. I remember it being just completely normal, unfortunately I've lost any talent of it (sign language), I lost it as soon as I went to school, this would be like any other kids. I did have callipers until I was eleven, by high school there wasn't really any sign that I'd had any illness. I did one of my films at film school on polio and my experience and the post-polio syndrome and what people experience now. I guess growing up I learned a lot about difference and different abilities.

I had a neighbourhood gang of friends and I don't remember much bullying or name calling or anything because of the callipers. I knew there were certain things I would have liked to have done but couldn't do. I didn't get a bike until I was eleven or twelve or something, I couldn't really ride one with callipers well. My main message from my father was 'you've just got to get on with it' and it was a survival mechanism I think for him and he did. He was one of the first disabled people employed at Holden when they opened up the first plant at Elizabeth. He used to go on the train every day from Prospect to Elizabeth and the big allowance was he was allowed him to knock off five minutes earlier than anyone else with a mate to be able to get onto the train to avoid the rush. He never had a guide dog. He used to be able to find his way around Adelaide on his own, he could tell people without directions where to go. How, I don't know.

A lot of influence in my life and attitudes came from my dad. In terms of disability and difference, in the message that it doesn't define anyone and all is not what it seems, just get on with it and overcome. I guess that has rubbed off. But as I got older and looked back on it my mother was certainly the enabler in all of that in quite intricate systems. When I look back at it I guess she'd be diagnosed as obsessive compulsive but it played out really well for their partnership in that all his clothes, for example, she would colour code which shirt and tie matched with threads so he wouldn't have to be dependent and ask all the time. He could go this is blue, this is red, that works, somebody told me those colours were alright. She would organise a lot of those sorts of things in this life.

My grandmother had died of breast cancer, and my maternal aunt was ill and my mother had nursed both of them, and then I had polio—I think that was probably enough so there were no other children. My father was one of eight and when I look at the family structures since then there are a lot of no children and one child families. Whether it was low fertility in the family or what, there were no big families. Several people didn't have children and several had one.

Growing up it was one of those great days in suburban Adelaide where kids sort of roamed in packs and you only come home at night for dinner, or tea as we would call it, we had one house one day and another house another day, riding bikes everywhere and having plenty of space to do what we wanted and no real threats of harm. Certainly no helicopter parents. We were expected to be out during the day and playing and having your own thing and not much accountability of what you were doing or where you were or whatever, which was a big sense of freedom. I guess, being an only child, I sort of look for that friendship and companionship maybe more than families who had brothers and sisters. My parents tried to foster a lot of that too. I had a very good children's playhouse that used to be an old, what they used to send cars in, old boxes, huge big boxes that have—in the gaps of the palings—have this oily paper that would stick and that was a waterproof thing so I had this large playhouse and it was great for kids to come and play in. And of course, we had the kangaroos which was another attraction.

1950s

LGBTIQ Culture Arises
Throughout the 1950s a gay community subculture developed with small bars and cafes becoming gay safe spaces. Police forces dedicated significant resources to tracking and arresting members of the LGBTIQ community.[5] Toward the end of the decade the Victoria police had close to a third of their vice squad raiding gay venues and entrapping gay men at known beats.[6]

David D

I grew up in Ashburton, Melbourne. 21st November 1949: I was an afterthought with my sisters thirteen and ten years older than me. Dad came back to the marriage when I came along. Mum was lazy and hard on my sisters. My parent's marriage was turbulent and a little violent. They slept in separate rooms with no cohabitation.

I had chronic asthma and eczema. Dad doted on me. Although fearful of his temper I adored him. For half of his working life he was a telegraphist and later during 1946 he became a senior Commonwealth public servant. He started his life as a Methodist but by 1930 he had become a communist. He did not drink or smoke or work much overtime. By the age of eight in 1958 he took me overseas by ship first-class on the *Strathaird* to Britain and Europe for six months and again at age 11 and 14.

I remember he told me a story that in 1929 he went to a Geelong-Richmond game at Richmond Oval, (a VFL game), where he said he started a riot and snuck out the back. He had been a boxer earlier in his life and although he had a fairly short fuse, I think he liked a bit of fun. His father was a PMG (Post-master General) linesman and they moved around a bit. Dad initially was born in Melbourne but they went up to Swan Hill and to Warrnambool. In Swan Hill dad got a job as a post office roustabout including working the manual phone equipment at night for the outback stations as the farmers were doing overseas business in England during the night. He eventually was able to become a telegraphist and many years later he became a senior Commonwealth public servant. Mum had been a seamstress with a fashion business called Le Roy Fashions in Flinders Lane where during the 1930s the Rag Trade was located in Melbourne. She always, throughout her life, loved making her own dresses and loved hats and things like that. She was extremely good-looking when she married Dad. I think she was actually working at the lolly counter for G.J. Coles when she met Dad. She used to dive under the counter for a mouthful of lollies! I think it was a physical attraction rather than an intellectual attraction when they married. They were both very good looking and mum was lazy with the housework and stuff like that and that resulted in an unhappy marriage. Dad was disappointed in that trait of my mum's and they ended up not cohabitating for most of their married life. Dad used to get very violent with Mum with arguments about her laziness with Dad pushing her around and hitting her. It upset me greatly. I was very introverted especially with my chronic asthma and eczema and my sisters being so much older. Dad left the marriage after my two sisters came along and somehow he went back to see mum and mum became pregnant with me. That brought dad back to the marriage. However, mum was very cruel with my sisters. She pushed them around to do work for her and criticised them a lot.

I was introverted and shy as a child with poor health. By 1955 we had a new local civic picture theatre, I used to go to the Saturday afternoon matinees. My sisters worked there and I always barracked for the Indians against the Cowboys. At age five I remember staring and admiring a boy my own age wearing an American sailors outfit.

In puberty 1963 I started to frequent the St Kilda Sea Baths where I was seduced by middle-aged men. It was not until age nineteen when I was in the second year of my law course and articled that I started to relate better with people. My overseas trips in 1958, 1961 and 1964 and competitive swimming from 1963 to 1974 brought great joy to me.

My first overseas trip in 1958 was very special. I was only eight and I developed a posh English accent in First Class aboard the *Strathaird* (launched 1931). As I say in my memoirs, I was dining separately as a child but on one occasion we had a meal with the grownups and dad made the point of telling me that some of the posh people on board would not be waitered by the coloured staff but in reality all people are equal and they should be accepted. I was as left-wing as dad was, probably even more so, and dad and my sister were members of the Communist Party. During this trip I went to the *Follies Berjere* in Paris and that was a pretty amazing experience. I can remember we were a little bit late and when Dad neglected to tip the usher, she started shining the torch in our eyes. I can remember vividly. I can remember some of the lovely ladies in the show. It broadened my horizons and gave me the taste for travel I've had all my life. My sister Dorothy said that I was a bit of a gypsy. In Yugoslavia in 1964 we initially got to Zagreb in the Cortina and when we went down for a meal dad had left his jacket on the bed. When we returned he found that the lining was unpicked from the jacket—very much the Cold War was going on. I sort of fantasised that Dad might have had a bit to do with espionage but that was just a fantasy.

On my first trip overseas to Bombay, or Mumbai as it is now known, was amazing. We were there at night climbing over people sleeping in the streets and we thought one or two of them were dead and when we came back on the way home in 1958 it was all cleaned up. The huge communal washing of clothes and the people defecating everywhere, it was a combination of a sweet and sour experience.

Dad loved Hyde Park Corner with the spruikers on a Sunday and he often remarked about the man who was singing 'where is my wandering boy tonight' and there were a lot of communists on Hyde Park Corner and we just loved it and I said to dad 'that man says the word sex and what's sex all about?' and he said 'don't worry about that'. No sex ed for me nor for my sisters and that was a big encumbrance because I wasn't aware about sexuality, didn't know anything about homosexuality, I thought I was just different. I thought maybe I was the only one apart from these men who were attracted to me. I was attracted to women but in the end I was more attracted to men. But I had some wonderful sexual relationships with three women in particular that I almost married.

Thomas

I was born in Katoomba New South Wales on 18 January 1951. My adopted father delivered me into this world. My parents had just escaped from the war in Europe, they fled from Czechoslovakia into Germany after Russia also invaded their country. They were offered to go to either England, Canada or Australia to migrate, luckily they chose Australia. When my parents arrived in Australia my father was sent to Sydney to work and my mother was sent to Parkes New South Wales, which is a fair way away. When I was born my father told my mother that if she kept me he would leave her. At this stage she did not speak English and didn't have a job so she was forced to give me up for adoption. My older sister was born on the ship over to Australia. Before I was born my adopted father, who was a doctor, actually delivered me and said to my mother if it is a boy I will keep him, which they did. I spent six months in hospital while everything was being arranged for my adoption. Of course you can't do it now, but I don't know if any money changed hands, that's what happened in those days.

I always felt as a young child (that) I was told I was privileged and I could have ended up in a boys home, and that made me feel special. My parents didn't hide the fact of my adoption. I don't think they told me until I was about ten or eleven but they didn't hide it. I had a better lifestyle with them, but they weren't a loving, kissing, cuddling, nurturing people, so I didn't get much affection. But I got well brought up and everything like that. I always thought that if I did the wrong thing they would send me to a boys home or something like that. It's just in the back of your mind, I think. I grew up in Wentworth Falls for the first five years, and Milton, and Newcastle This is all in New South Wales. And then to Berry for the next five years. Afterwards we moved to several places in Sydney, and then to Moss Vale, which is about a hundred miles from Sydney in the southern highlands, where I completed my school years. My adoptive parents gave me a good upbringing, but they were never really affectionate. I never remember being cuddled or kissed much as a child. My older sister was also adopted and when I was five my adoptive parents had a son of their own. He was spoiled rotten and me and my sister felt a bit left out, but that's what happens when they have kids of their own.

I bonded with my father's sister Aunty Hope, who was also my godmother. I always felt welcome and happy at her house. She welcomed me into the family. My father's family was also very strict and they were all teachers and doctors, and there wasn't a lot of emotional stuff—I didn't find—in their family, except for this one aunty, my Aunty Hope.

Michael

My childhood in the 1950s centred around school, the Methodist Church, and the wireless. I had no interest then in competitive sport or pop music, and remain so. Elvis Presley and the banality of 'How Much Is That Doggie in the Window' did nothing for me. The wireless, through the ABC, was where I developed an interest in classical music—Italian songs, some opera and chamber music. My parents, even though they were members of the Methodist Church, weren't particularly religious. They were attracted (as I became) by its social activities and a sense of community. There were Friday night youth club, the occasional hay ride, with the annual picnic and the Sunday school anniversary staged as major events. Sundays involved morning church and Sunday school, with Christian Endeavour in the afternoon. My parents did not own a car (second hand) until 1969, and thus growing up we walked everywhere: to school, to church and going to the shops (some distance away) involved a lot of walking and carrying purchases home in all weather.

I grew up in a very loving and supportive family. My mother was the disciplinarian, making use of the occasional 'strap'. Mum looked after the finances and I suppose I was mildly frightened of her. My father would do anything to avoid conflict. He never hit me and only once ever raised his voice to me, when as a kid I walked on his freshly laid cement! Growing up on a struggling soldier settlement farm, he had had to leave school early during the Depression. He was very clever with his hands and making things. He was a good man in every sense. He married in 1941 when he was twenty-one and my mother twenty. Stereotypes suggest that gay guys have conflicts with their parents or their fathers in particular but I never really experienced that at all. Though I do recall having a fierce argument with my mother at age sixteen when after living in Adelaide for a few month, I wanted to wear my new stylish blue cravat to a church social function. My first display of youthful independence? I just could not fathom her objection!

I left home at sixteen to complete my Leaving Honours at Adelaide Boys High school and boarded with an aunt. I was never conscious of being poor until I came to the city. I just never seemed to have lacked anything considered essential materially growing up, but on a single income there was little money to spend on books. My parents were fortunate in 1941 to buy a dilapidated house (built in 1857) with a loan from his employer and only sold it in 2010. We had a cow, grew vegetables and fruit trees, and kept chickens. One of my chores as a kid was churning butter and I learnt to catch, kill and pluck a chicken for Sunday lunch, but never mastered milking the cow.

My few friends were from school and church social groups. I experienced the odd bit of bullying at school but nothing that scarred me. Attending a small country school I was reasonably bright but I wouldn't say a highflier, I had to work hard at school and was more at home in the humanities than the sciences, and manifestly inept at woodwork. What seeped through most from my father was his political attitudes. He was a committed Labor man and trade union member. I was long nurtured on the saintliness of Ben Chifley in the new Menzies era. And he took me to my first political meeting when the SA Labor Leader of the Opposition visited our town—I must (obviously) have been showing an interest in politics at fifteen or sixteen. I know that he flirted with Communism in the 1940s and I still have his copy of the Communist Manifesto with pencilled annotations. My initial political beliefs, largely retained, took root then in the 1950s, but most were developed in the 1960s in response to the Vietnam War.

One of the things that did influence me in 1950s were some of my teachers. I remember in 1956 my English teacher interrupted her lesson on the Wind in the Willows and switched on the wireless in the classroom. I didn't understand at the time but she made it sound so important—Mr Menzies was talking about the Suez Crisis because he had been an envoy for the British Government to Colonel Nasser in Cairo and obviously it was an important announcement in the speech he was making. I don't remember the content of it but it gave me an interest in the wider world and as a thirteen-year-old it had a dramatic effect on me.

Later I applied for a teaching scholarship, which took me to the city in 1960 to do Leaving Honours.

Gabby

I'd describe my upbringing as good, perfect. My upbringing was by a naval background. My father was a naval officer, a petty officer. Mum was in it as well. We moved here when I was about two years of age, so I had a good life. There wasn't anything I needed or wanted or desired. I had a controlled life where 7:30-8:00 you're in bed and that was really the only regimented part I had growing up. I always knew there was something—always in my mind, in my body—I knew there was something that was different to everybody else. I tried to fit in. I'd go play football, I'd do the soccer, I'd do the rugby and I did the cricket, but I never really fit in. I always thought I was an outsider because there was a mismatch of some kind and I could never put my finger on that mismatch. One of my primary school teachers I still have a friendship with. She knows me now after transition and she said now it makes sense, now she's seen me transition it makes sense why I was like I was, because in the era

I grew up there were no gays. If you were gay you were ostracised much more than you are now—ridiculed, bullied massively.

I always lived in the Elizabeth area. I had close friends but not very many, a small network. I was always the odd one out. I was the stronger one, the louder one. I wouldn't let anyone bully anyone. A friend of mine, Philip, he said I was always the protector—I wouldn't let a little kid get beaten up by three other people, or whatever. I would always step in, even with the issues I was dealing with. I'm very protective, I don't like people taking advantage of other people. Even in my own life I'll have instances where I'll be really, really offended by someone and really angry if they have done something really bad to me, but if I know within myself that they are not equal in their ability, to do things or handle things then I regard attacking anyone or being aggressive towards them as bullying. I'm not saying that I'm better than them, but that's the way I look at it. I can't do that. I can't bully someone. I can't be aggressive to someone who's weaker than I am. I believe in equality. You can think you're better but you're not, everybody has their faults.

When it comes to who inspires me—this one gets me—Christine Jorgensen. Knowing her story at the age I did. And I knew myself, she was hope, there was a chance, there was a way. Knowing about her, I knew as a little kid growing up of the ladyboys in Thailand. I knew they were around and I knew that they were women but women with penises, and I know I didn't hate my body, I didn't hate my penis. I loved who I was but I wasn't necessarily happy with who I was. I didn't disrespect my body in the sense that I didn't want to self-mutilate, or cut it off or anything of that nature, but I knew I could change. I knew there was a way I could be complete like how I am today.

You've got to understand I grew up knowing I was different. I perceive myself as knowing from around about five or six that I wasn't meant to be a boy. I kept that to myself. My mum caught me at seven years of age in the corridor all dressed up in my sister's clothes, make up, shoes and everything. I knew from a very early age from listening to stories about ladyboys, but when Christine Jorgensen's story came to light (1952 *New York Daily News* Front Page) I knew there was someone who could go that way, who could have the operation. You could change. You didn't have to live that way. That was TV and radio when she came out, and it was spoken about. You knew there was someone like that around.

Hugh

At the same time New South Wales didn't decriminalise gays until 1984, that is nine years after South Australia. The penalties, the possible penalties that a judge could impose (every state had different laws at that stage) the penalties that the judge could impose on gay men who indulged in gay sex in Sydney at that time were up to twelve years in prison.

This discouraged Michael Kirby and also discouraged me, especially because whenever a gay person was arrested it was printed on the front page of the newspaper. The outstanding case, that shocked me to the core, was Claudio Arrau, the famous Chilean pianist, one of the greatest interpreters of Beethoven in the world. He was arrested by a police agent provocateur. This means a good-looking young policeman in plain clothes, who goes onto beats and pretends to be interested in guys, usually older men, and leads them on. Then, at the crucial moment he says, 'You're under arrest'. That's what happened to Claudio Arrau and what was shocking for me about it was not just that it was on the front page of the newspaper, but that it was on the front page of the *Sydney Morning Herald*. Now, the *Sydney Morning Herald* was a family newspaper and was the best quality paper in Sydney. We took it every day and most other families did too in our social class, but they published relentlessly every tiny detail of that case. They crucified poor Claudio and really made a scapegoat of him. It was a triumph for the Philistines, and my father was a Philistine, who believed what was preached from the church pulpits. In other words what many churches, including ours, were preaching then was that gay people are perverted, that they're mentally unstable and that they're unclean. When you get that pushed at you every

Sunday, or every other Sunday, that makes you hate yourself. That can take a long time to get over.

So what I was feeling after seeing what happened to Claudio was more than anything else that 'I must hide this'. Because I was into music—I was into the arts big time—and he was one of my idols. To see this happen to him was absolutely horrifying. The other thing I thought, as well as 'I must hide this', was 'I don't deserve to be happy. I'm such a miserable, degenerate sort of person that I cannot possibly be happy in my life. And even if I were I wouldn't deserve to be'. That again is a very powerful negative thing to be telling yourself. There was no gay counselling at that stage for anybody and no gay organisations to speak of. I'm talking about the 50s.

That went on, feeling that way and trying to hide in a corner but, of course, the hormones were still raging inside me, so I played around a bit, always racked by guilt. Until my gap year in 1952, when I went to Europe and to England and a small town in Yorkshire, where a friend of my mother's, Miss Richardson, was the deputy headmistress of the local high school. She was the perfect English gentlewoman. She was a vicar's daughter, she had an immensely dignified carriage. She was not all that tall, but she looked tall by the way she carried herself. She had the most perfect manners I have ever seen in anybody, man or woman. And the usual things: tweeds, sensible shoes, and pearls. She was a churchwarden. I couldn't believe it, because she also lived with her partner, but nobody called them partner in those days, they called them 'friends'. Her partner was the senior maths mistress at the school. Nobody raised an eyebrow. They lived in a beautiful two-storey house with a lovely garden. Later on she went on to become the mayor of the town. No one said anything, and I thought, 'Ye gods, you can live a decent, productive life and still be gay'.

That was a total eye-opener to me. She was the first person I knew of who was openly gay. I mean there had been overheard whispers about other people, friends and relatives, my father gossiping after a whisky or two about one of the men he played golf with, one of my aunts, one of the bachelors at church, and so on, but nobody we knew was openly gay and no-one ever spoke of it in front of the children. I was still considered a child at that stage, at seventeen.

I came back to Sydney in 1953 and did my university degree and then teacher training—of course all this gay consciousness happens while the rest of your life is happening too. I didn't get along with my father at all, so first of all, when I was fifteen, my parents had sent me away to boarding school to stop all the arguments. Then as soon as I could, as soon as I was on my teaching college allowance, I moved out of home and got myself a room somewhere else. It wasn't very comfortable and I didn't do anything particularly striking, but it just made me feel independent.

I graduated in 1958, but was on a bond for another three years. I was teaching secondary school. I actually was trained for French and English, but finished up teaching lots of other things, because I was sent to the country. People still on their bond often ended up at the places where nobody else wanted to go. I taught things that you could look up the night before, like history and so on. It wasn't too bad, because in the country we made our own fun, but to admit you were gay in a small country town would have been social and professional suicide. Anyway, as soon as my bond was finished I got out of teaching, because I really wasn't cut out for it.

1960s

Political and Police Movements on the March
Homosexuality (Pinks) and communism (Reds) were considered closely linked as threats to national security. Such fears were developed from propaganda coming out of the United States that portrayed homosexual people as a security risk who would 'more likely be loyal to each other than to their country.'[7]

Prime Minister Menzies didn't outlaw LGBTIQ people being employed in government jobs, but he did enforce a directive that LGBTIQ people couldn't access confidential information.

Stonewall Riots
28th June 1969 marked an impromptu uprising from within the LGBTIQ community. They took to the streets in response to ongoing police brutality which culminated in a raid on the Stonewall Inn. Throughout the 60s there were many police raids, which clubs combatted through police pay offs, hidden bottles of alcohol (to circumvent licensing issues), separate discreet meeting rooms, and light signals for patrons to stop dancing, touching and hide 'effeminate' traits.

On the night of June 28th there was a raid on the Stonewall Inn, and this time the community responded. There are contested reports of who 'threw the first brick' but what is found in police and witness reports is that transgender people, people of colour, and drag queens instigated a struggle when being arrested that occurred while the crowd grew to several hundred (far more than those in the bar during the raid). Marsha P. Johnson and Sylvia Rivera were part of the uprising and continued to be activists within the LGBTIQ community until their deaths.

The riots continued for a second night. Pride marches were held on this day the following year to commemorate the riots.

Philip

I was born only about half a kilometre from here (home), and for most of the time I've lived here in Adelaide. My parents were markets gardeners, but then because land became so expensive and property taxes became so expensive they had to sell that and just get ordinary jobs. So, it was an ordinary suburban family upbringing.

We'll get straight to the part of me being gay. That didn't really matter, because overshadowing that at the time was the financial crisis of my oldest brother. So, whatever my middle brother and I did was just shut up and get out of our parents' way, because there was a big bushfire burning with my oldest brother. He had a farm, but my parents had signed as guarantors for the farm. The problem was that he didn't make his repayments to the bank, so each of my parents had to work three jobs to pay back to the bank for my oldest brother's debts. He then disassociated himself from them and had shocking arguments. I could have dyed my hair green. I could have grown long curly fingernails and they just wouldn't have had time to notice. Same for my middle brother. It was very much, 'At least they're okay. At least they don't want our money'. So it wasn't an issue. I'm the youngest son of the three sons. That's why I say, for me money is incredibly important: when you see it wreaking havoc in a family and when it becomes our money crisis like that. The sexuality, I think, just goes out the window, and other things go out the window, because my parents knew they had to pay back the bank for their own survival, or they would lose their own house.

They were exhausted as well, with the work and with the arguments with him about all that debt. So they just didn't have eyes in their heads and or brains in the head enough to notice what we were doing. Neither of us was particularly inclined to do anything particularly wrong, so they just breathed a sigh of relief that we were okay.

In terms of getting a boyfriend: I had noticed men from my earliest age. You know, women just didn't interest me. It was okay, I knew women existed, but they didn't interest me sexually at all, but men fascinated me. Things like hairy legs or whatever it might be on an older man, just fascinated me, the whole thing. I'm talking when I was six, seven years old.

But then in terms of getting a first boyfriend, that was when I was fourteen. Again my parents didn't seem to worry terribly much about that. We were about twelve or thirteen. We'd built cubby houses at each other's house and used to sleep over together, and they knew something was going on there. But one time, when mum came home I was chasing my boyfriend around the sitting room naked and he was naked too, and we both had erections. She knew then for sure that we were gay. She knew it wasn't just two boys who are living in the same area. That's when she knew, and after that it was all out in the open. I don't know if my parents were okay with it or not. I just think it was another thing that happened that day, a particularly hectic day between shifts at work. It was just an event that happened that day when she just happened to walk in, after one job, and saw her third son running around the sitting room naked, but then she had to go out to work again.

She knew and my father knew, of course, that the guy who lived around the road, Colin, was gay as well. It was some years later that dad said to me, 'I saw Colin, I was driving the cab the other night and Colin got in, and now Colin's a girl'. And I thought, 'What's happened here?'.

It was years after we'd broken up. It was just interesting, dad knew all along and he'd followed Colin's progress. I wouldn't say there was any friction to do with my sexuality in the family.

Hugh

So in 1962 I joined the ABC as an education producer, which was my dream job. I loved it. Right from the start I did music programs for schools, which at first were pretty old hat. I worked towards changing that. After I'd done my probation training in Sydney with the ABC I got sent to Perth. We're now in the early 60s, actually 1962. I was still in the church, believe it or not, but I was. I was still in the choir and all that, and I met another young guy called Keith, aged twenty-two in the church and we became best friends. We weren't lovers but we were really close and he was a clever Economics student. He was also very sensitive and he fell in love with an older man. I say an older man, but I mean when you're twenty-two, thirty-four seems old. My friend had really strict parents, also in the church. A jealous rival threatened to tell his parents what was going on and so... he... shot himself—It was... such a waste... a terrible, terrible waste...

After the tragedy with my friend, I left the church. The minister said to me, 'You can go on being gay and still be in the church, provided you don't do anything about it'. And I said, 'That's like you can be a dog, but never bark'.

So I left, and soon I found a really nice group of young people called the Guild of Young Artists, who were interested in the same kind of things as me. We put on shows and concerts and generally had a great time. But I wasn't active sexually. I hadn't reached that degree of confidence and self-acceptance after Keith's death. It had really shocked me. Also, bear in mind that gay sex in WA was not decriminalised until 1989, fourteen years after SA.

The ABC sent me to Hobart next, in 1965, and in some way that was great, because it was such a small place that I was allowed to do all kind of things that I would not have had the chance to do in a bigger place. I experimented with the music programs, working with a gifted young teacher who'd just returned from studying in Austria. I produced a musical (for which I won an award), produced a three act play, played lots of roles on stage (including the lead in *A Man for All Seasons* and took principal roles in Gilbert and Sullivan musicals. I was also in constant demand as a tenor soloist in oratorio. So I was lucky enough to perform in works by Haydn, Handel, Mozart, Britten and Berlioz. I also appeared in two operas and joined The Renaissance Consort. I remained soloist with the latter for twelve years, performing in Melbourne, Canberra and Adelaide as well as Tasmania. We were also broadcast on ABC Radio and featured in the Proms. I was a big fish in a small pond.

The drawback was that Hobart basically was a police state, as far as gays were concerned. They didn't decriminalise homosexuality until twenty-two years after South Australia, in 1997, and even then they were forced to by the United Nations.

In the late sixties there were still all sorts of injustices and unpleasant things associated with the laws against gays. One of them was blackmail and another of them was that, if your enemies really disliked you, or had some particular grudge against you, they could denounce you to the police. In other words, they could tell the police what you are up to. For instance if you owed them a lot of money and couldn't pay them they would tell the police that you were gay and then the police would come, catch you in the act and put you in jail. In Tasmania the penalties were higher than anywhere else. They were up to twenty-one years and a greater proportion of gays were in prison there than in any other state.

The same thing applied to newspapers. There were two really nasty cases, both people I admired in the arts. One was Max Oldaker, who had been a big star of J.C. Williamsons in the 40s and 50s in musical comedy. He still appeared occasionally on the Sydney stage. He was arrested in Launceston. Max was one of those people who can charm the leg off an iron pot. He was a very elegant and stylish man and he had what I can only describe as glamour. He did a lot of voluntary work for amateur theatre in Tasmania, but it all counted for nothing.

The other guy who was exposed on the front pages of the newspaper was a handsome tenor with the Australian Opera, who had come to Hobart to star in a show. He was arrested one night while he was on the beat. It was a terrible thing, because apart from anything else he was married, and he was also a very fine artist. It was terrible to me, who admired them, Max and Claudio, to see these very artistic, very talented people being crucified on the front pages of the newspaper, one after another, with no comeback. The fact that these guys were exposed meant that they could lose their job, they could lose their reputation, they did lose their reputation. They were fined rather than imprisoned, but if the judge wished to he could have imprisoned them. It was a very nasty situation. This is what I mean by saying Tasmania was a police state.

They were just starting to have gay community groups when I was towards the end of my time in Tasmania. I was there for nine years, and what the police would do is come around while those meetings were on, they were always told when they were on, (there was no shortage of informers) and they would take the number plates of the cars that were attending so they knew who was there. Dreadful things were said in the Tasmanian Parliament about gay people. They actually said worse things in the Parliament than they said in the pulpit when I was a child, and they went on saying them. It was all reported in the media, and that helped inflame public opinion further against gays.

I had various affairs down there, none of which was very satisfactory. I did become completely infatuated, when I was doing a lot of amateur theatre, with a young guy who was in the same show as me. He was a dancer and he was a final year Teacher's College student and very sexually experienced. I really wanted it to go somewhere and I wanted to be with him. He had a great sense of humour, red hair, and he was just lovely to watch, he moved beautifully. Later on I found some things about him that weren't so pleasant, but I was totally bananas about him.

David D

Doug Wade was probably the best full forward ever in 1964 and he was a very handsome man and my cousin Daryl took me to the training one night, I think it was a Thursday night, and we went into the clubrooms and there I saw Doug Wade in the bath fully resplendent with his wonderful attributes and that really stuck in my mind. I loved going to the footy with dad. The handsome men were a big attraction for me. For twenty-five years we went pretty well every Saturday. It meant bonding with dad and it meant I spent some quality time with him and we had a common passion for the game. It was wonderful. There was that routine with the Geelong relatives on Saturdays, and as I said in 1929 Dad had been following Geelong and started a riot in Richmond. He had a long association. I think his dad could have been a Geelong supporter because his dad was born on the Torquay Road out of Geelong so I think there was a long Geelong history there.

During the days of conscription and the Vietnam War dad and I and my sisters created a massive banner entitled 'Down with US Puppets' with a depiction of our Prime Minister, US President, and President Ky. We marched in an enormous Melbourne protest against the South Vietnamese President Ky while he was visiting in 1967. In 1974 I joined the fledging Melbourne Gay Society and frequented steam bars in a basement opposite the Hotel Australia and not long after that the Caulfield sauna.

Michael

I failed my first year of university in all four subjects though I did pass my Teacher's Collage subjects. I was captured by fundamentalist evangelical Christianity in 1961. This evolved and was nurtured through my membership and active participation in the Evangelical Union, which shaped my life for the next ten years.

I'm not attributing my failure in 1961 to this religious commitment, but I was still quite immature and burdened with heavy coursework and I tended to read a lot other than the required studies as well as prepare myself for examinations. It was however a watershed moment. I had earlier failed Latin in 1959, which I needed to matriculate and was forced to sit for a supplement to be able to take up my teaching scholarship. Part of the reason I'd failed was that I was the only student taking Latin with the busy headmaster of a small school. He could only teach me a couple of days a week in his office and I had to rely on his set of written notes. This left me with a shaky grasp of grammar and a range of often obscure vocabulary. Fortunately I was to learn from these painful experiences of failure and I did receive a free university education that doesn't fall to the current generation. My university education resulted in two things for me: I went out teaching not having completed my BA degree so I had to complete it while I was teaching, which was not always easy; and it also sowed the seeds of the idea of what I most wanted to do with my life, to train as a church missionary.

At the end of my first year of teaching I spent all of the summer vacation (December 1965-1966) in the Eastern Highlands of New Guinea, organised by the evangelical InterVarsity Fellowship as guests of Summer Institute of Linguistics/Wycliffe Bible Translators. I was just twenty-two and it was a life-changing experience. I was isolated in a grass hut on the side of a mountain and worked to flatten out an airstrip for safer landings. I was supervising 'natives' as they were then described, paying them a shilling a day to work with shovels and rollers. Becoming filthy dirty at the end of each day I'd go down to a river, strip off and sit on a rock and splash water to clean up. And then on the weekends I walked a couple of miles through tall kunai grass to the village where there was a warm bucket shower and home-cooked meals from a Canadian missionary family were provided.

This experience shaped my next few years, finishing my BA degree in 1969, resigning from the Education Department and then embarking on a Bachelor of Divinity degree in 1970, for which an initial degree was a prerequisite, taken externally through the Melbourne university affiliate, Ormond College, from the Methodist theological college in Adelaide.

1970s

LGBTIQ Campaign Groups Formed and Organised
In the early 1970s an array of LGBTIQ support, protest and advocacy groups spawned following the Stonewall riots. The LGBTIQ community became more organised and visible over this period, particularly in urban areas. Protesting and lobbying increased the recognition of LGBTIQ rights and resulted in a range of changes, such as legislative reform decriminalising homosexual sex acts and the declassification of homosexuality as a mental illnesses. Prominent openly LGBTIQ people began to win positions as public officials, including the likes of Harvey Milk in 1977.

Queer groups began to form in major Australian cities from the 1970s. Whilst a number of these focussed on community support, the Campaign Against Moral Persecution (CAMP) was the first to focus on political activism. CAMP was first established in Sydney in July 1970, released its first publication in November 1970, and held its first public meeting in February 1971.[8] The organisation had 2000 members within a year, and formed branches on university campuses in Sydney and Adelaide. These groups confronted media misinformation surrounding homosexuality and issues of sexuality, and in the process established an informal LGBTIQ network around Australia.

CAMP coordinated their first political protest in October 1971 during a Liberal Party pre-selection where Jim Cameron, right-wing politician stood against Tom Hughes, who was the Liberal government's federal Attorney-General at the time and in favour of limited legislative reforms on homosexuality. The group then decided to demonstrate outside Liberal Party headquarters.

Dr Duncan's Death[9]

The murder of Adelaide University law lecturer Dr George Duncan by elite South Australian police vice officers became a flash point that helped drive through the legislation that would decriminalise homosexuality in the state. Dr Duncan was at a well-known beat by the Torrens River on 10th May 1972 when he was set upon and thrown into the river where he subsequently drowned. The murder made national headlines, and while details of those responsible are well publicised, there wasn't sufficient evidence for conviction and a trial was never held.

Following the murder, South Australian Premier Don Dunstan, a gay man himself, began strengthening the push for legislation to decriminalise homosexuality, which would eventually lead South Australia to become the first Australian state to do so and for the law to come into event in 1975.

AMA Removes Homosexuality from List of Illnesses and Disorders

Prior to 1973 the American Psychiatric Association (APA), as perhaps the most influential authority on mental health, classified homosexuality as a psychological disorder, which was reflected in the Diagnostic and Statistical Manual of Mental Disorders (DSM-II), and condoned aversion therapy as a viable treatment. This position attracted the attention of gay activists, who protested numerous APA conferences. Alongside protests, activists presented the APA with decades of research and data on human sexual behaviour by Alfred Kinsey and Evelyn Hooker, and organised for Dr John E. Fryer, a gay man and psychiatrist member of the APA, to publicly address the organisation in 1972. He spoke anonymously from behind a wig, face mask and voice distorter due to the very real risk to his career, and told the APA that their profession considered him to have a sexual deviation and was prejudiced against gay people. The APA voted to no longer classify homosexuality as a psychological disorder in December 1973, which was reflected in subsequent printings of the DSM-II. They were preceded by the Australian and New Zealand College of Psychiatry, who declared the same in October 1973. Other peak medical bodies followed suit,[10] along with the World Health Organisation, who eventually removed homosexuality as a disorder in the ninth edition of the International Classification of Diseases (ICD-9) published in 1992.

South Australia Passed a National First

Legislation to decriminalise consensual sex between adult men was first introduced in the South Australian parliament as a private member's bill by Murray Hill in 1972 following the death of Dr George Duncan. The bill was eventually passed in 1975 after several failed attempts.

Following the decriminalisation of homosexuality in South Australia, the state became an extradition option for states that prosecuted homosexual sex acts. One infamous case involved a gay male couple in Victoria who were raided in their own home and subsequently convicted under anti-homosexuality laws. In sentencing they were offered the option of imprisonment or deportation to South Australia. The couple chose the latter.[11]

The First Sydney Mardi Gras

24th June 1978 saw in the first Sydney Mardi Gras that was a march as part of international Gay Solidarity Celebrations. The events were in support of events and rights campaign that extended from the Stonewall Riots of 1969. The initial, peaceful and colourful celebrations quickly turned when New South Wales police confiscated the lead float and arrested the driver.[12] What began as a few hundred people heading up Oxford Street to read telegrams of support tipped over 1,500 following the police intervention. Over fifty people were later arrested, many beaten in police cells. A lot of the charges where eventually dropped but not after the local newspapers outed the names and employment of many involved. The Sydney Gay and Lesbian Mardi Gras continues today as the largest event of its kind in Australia. The original marchers are now referred to as the 78'ers.

Mahamati

I identify as lesbian. I had experiences with girls when I was quite young and a part of the neighbourhood kids and I'm not sure how or what that was. I quickly got the message that this wasn't supposed to be okay and that most people aim for boyfriends. I think I'm a bisexual lesbian or that sort of label because I got married when I was very young. I was eighteen (in 1964) and I was in love. I met David at a youth club. My parents weren't church goers but I sought it out because that's where the youth clubs were and that's where the activity was and that's where the dances were. These were things I wanted to be involved with and I met David at a mutual Anglican church, St Mary's in Halifax Street in the city, and both our youth groups were there doing whatever good works it was that youth clubs do.

I think I was only sixteen when we met. I think I really wanted to get away from home, that was a big driver (for marriage). I wanted more freedom and more independence. I believe I was genuinely in love with David. I know we were divorced for longer than we were married. We were married nineteen years. We're still on quite good terms and in terms of our kids and parenting. He was still in teachers training college when I met him. Then he was teaching. We got married in 1964 and very shortly after the things we were involved with at St Mary's children's home evolved quite quickly. This sort of feeds into the social justice things, or whatever you'd like to call it, that I've grown up with. We used to do a lot with the children there, we'd take them away for weekends. David's parents had a hobby farm up in Clare. it wasn't called a hobby farm then but that's what it was. So we'd often take kids away for the weekend and two of the girls from the children's home were flower girls at our wedding. One of them, Barbara, we adopted in the end.

At first we fostered her. It was the time when a lot of the social welfare laws were changing thanks to Don Dunstan and there was some new law that if the parents were subpoenaed and didn't come to court then the court had the right to make the decision about the child's future. We were advised by the child welfare department at the time that if we wanted to adopt her we should consider doing that but I had to wait until I was twenty-one because there wasn't a natural age gap. We would have had to have her at thirteen for there to be a natural age gap and I was horrified that people could think that I had her at thirteen and hidden her away.

We had Barb, we were living in Adelaide, David was teaching at North Adelaide School and he was an extraordinary teacher and at that time a lot of kids came from post-war migration and if they were older and didn't speak English they were put back into grade seven so we would have Italian and Greek boys who were fourteen in grade six, grade seven. He used to do a lot with them, he used to run a surf board thing down at the beach and kids would all come down on the weekend and things you would never do with teaching now. He had a flat in North Adelaide before we were married and all the kids would come around and be playing darts and things you would never do in terms of duty of care or worry about as a teacher, piling fifteen kids into the Volkswagen to get to football.

Travis

This is the stuff that seems quite straightforward that's really difficult to answer, but my upbringing was I think really unremarkable, two parents, a brother and a sister, nice grandparents, no horrible events, no nasty people. I went to a state primary school in the 1960s and that was fine. We lived in England for eighteen months in London when I was ten or eleven and then I went to a private high school. Under zoning I would have gone to the local state technical high school, where the academic standard was probably not what I was capable of and I probably wouldn't have been academically stretched, and I wouldn't have made it to university from the local high school. I would have wound up a tradesman, probably then a lot richer than I am now. I had no say in it (schooling). I assumed I was going to the local high school and a friend who was going to the private school and said, 'you're going there too' and I said, 'no that wouldn't be true' but turned out to be true, selected not on the basis of the status or cost or religion but on the basis of it's a more convenient bus route and on the other side of town.

Friends? Did I have friends? I'm just thinking back on primary school: nothing really. I got on well with the other kids, however I was a bit isolated because I preferred academics and reading to playing sports and that was a bit isolating. I tended to get along better with the girls but had fun friendships with local children up the street. I don't recall anyone being particularly close but I got on with most people. I was in an all-boys high school and did fall in love a few times, which was not reciprocated, so they got called friendships. I had a good friend at school who I wasn't attracted to, and he was just a really nice, interesting, intelligent person.

I was academic. I was in the top five of the school throughout the five high school years. The outstanding top boy by some margin—the brightest, most academically achieving boy in the place—was gay. and I never knew until I met him years and years later. Not knowing about him in school brings me a complete sense of lost opportunity. I wasn't attracted to him and I wouldn't have gone there, but we would have made a great team and we would have had a lot of fun subverting the dominant ideology in a homophobic Christian school, where this bright boy had a boyfriend at one stage. The boyfriend mysteriously disappeared from the school and was never heard of again. The teachers actively worked on keeping them separate in the schoolyard and then the following year the other boy didn't come back to the school. So jumping back, this is what I found out years later and it enhanced my image of the school as being primarily concerned with its own image and its care for its students was, in my view, minimal. There was one teacher in particular onto whom I think I loved to project this fatherly caring supportive image and he was out-and-out homophobic, and I think he would have made my life hell.

The school had a scout trip and it had military cadets at the school itself. From the second year of high school you had to be in one or the other, so that was 1972 to 75. That was the deal, there was scouts and cadets. I presumed it was about discipline and skill learning more than going camping. Of course the scouts had the gay reputation, definitely in the 70s. It wasn't so much about the leaders abusing the kids, it was about the kids having sex with each other, and this was reputed to happen in the scouts. Now, I did not have a sexual experience with anyone at school or in the Scouts, and if anyone had made any moves on me I missed it. And although I wanted to, I certainly didn't make any moves on anyone else, so there was no action in the scouts for me. But I found out later from this other boy that in the cadets, it was a different story. That's where all the action was happening.

I will relate to you an episode that happened in the scouts. I seriously can't remember if this was a scout thing or just a school thing and it does stick in my mind about what happened and what didn't. There was a particular teacher who was a scout leader and he was probably in his late 50s maybe 60s when I was at school, and he had a reputation among the boys for liking to touch up the boys. I was in a small group conducted by this teacher doing first aid training, so we were learning how to stop bleeding and put on bandages, nothing as advanced as CPR. I would have been about fourteen perhaps and we were in this group and somebody puts a bandage on my knee, and this teacher inspected the bandage by rubbing his face up my leg and I remember thinking that's weird. I didn't particularly enjoy it but it wasn't particularly disgusted or frightened or horrified by it. I just found it weird and it was consistent with what I heard about this teacher. It simply did not occur to me to discuss this with anyone, and really it wasn't like what we hear about abuse from teachers, like we are seeing now. It's not particularly that was I was frightened or embarrassed or didn't think I would be believed or anything like that. I didn't tell any of the other boys because everybody knew it wasn't really any different from anything I heard and I don't think it occurred to any of us to tell other teachers or the principal or parents. I don't think we assumed they knew and I can't recall what I thought. Possibly part of it was the teacher was a nice guy, it was odd but it wasn't particularly offensive or frightening, and I think probably we all liked him and we wouldn't have wanted to get him into trouble.

But there was no formal agreement, never 'we're going to look after him', it was all unspoken and what goes beyond that is speculation.

All the nice, charismatic, in some way fatherly type teachers I wound up with a really low opinion of. When I was more senior in the school I wanted to be formally accredited as a scout leader, and one teacher who was also a scout leader blocked it. He didn't say why but I think he was onto my sexuality. He showed me a letter that was written to another teacher cancelling his accreditation as a scout leader. He just showed it to me, and I wondered what is he getting at? Through other sources I think that teacher was found in the sack with one of the kids, and so as seemed to be the response to such situations in those days the kid got moved on to another school pretty fast. I think he was the one person who was onto my sexuality. Ultimately he wasn't supportive at all. He was way more concerned about the systems, the integrity of the church, and didn't care about individuals, was my impression. In the end he left to go into the priesthood and then this military type scout leader took over and he couldn't see what all the fuss had been about so he just pushed through my accreditation as scout leader. I think I did well there and I didn't fiddle with any kids.

I think my Aunt, she is probably the one who more than anyone else gave me subtle messages that you can do what you want to do, you can be what want to be, be the best of yourself. So she was probably a major influence, and when I eventually came out in my thirties, she was the one who didn't bat an eyelid: 'good, glad we got that out of the way'. She was a dancer, so even in the 60s perhaps met the occasional gay. She died a couple of years ago of Alzheimer's, which was terribly, terribly sad. My grandmother, my dad's mother, was a pretty powerful influence on me as well. She is probably responsible for my disciplined approach to finances and some of my hoarding tendencies. That's what happens with depression kids. It's taken me a long time to get around to 'that's not working properly anymore, replace it. I don't need that anymore get rid of it. I'm not using that throw it out'. I suspect she was onto me as well.

Hugh

So, I came back to Sydney in 1972 for my holidays, staying with my mother. My parents had been divorced by this stage. I went to a show, a musical, with her and my sister and her new husband, who was a doctor. Musicals are often so corny and sentimental, but one scene really got to me. It was about people being parted and I just couldn't stop crying. It was totally unlike me, I mean, you won't believe it after my outburst a minute ago over Keith's death in Perth, but it was very, very unusual for me.

The next morning, over the marmalade, my mother said to me, 'Is there something you want to tell me that I should know?' and so the whole story came out. Then she said, 'I'm your mother so I suspected something like this, but I always hoped that you would marry a woman.' (these are her very words) 'I'd hoped that you would marry a woman who was not much interested in sex'.

I couldn't believe she could be as cruel and as ruthless as that, to both me and the woman. She had in fact encouraged a couple of possible liaisons like that, one when I was teaching in the country. So later she said, 'I'm going to send you to a psychiatrist. Pat's husband, John, has recommended somebody'. Thank God! John had recently graduated, so he knew a lot of other guys who had recently graduated and the one he recommended was in Sydney at the Royal North Shore hospital. He was enlightened enough to say to me words similar to what Bob Brown's psychiatrist said to him, 'The only thing you have to do is to accept yourself'.

This was at a time when some of the old school of psychiatrists were still using shock treatment and still saying that gays could be cured and that it was a mental illness and so I was terrified that all this would happen to me, but none of it did. It was so wonderful to hear. It was like freedom.

Anyway, I went back to Tasmania, and just before I left Sydney my sister-in-law said to me, 'I see the gays in South Australia have taken over the government,' (because Don Dunstan came to power in 1970) 'and they're doing a good job.'

I thought, 'I want to go there.'

Philip

Easily the biggest influence about what I should do with my life would have been my grandparents. My grandfather had a business and he was interested in the share market, and that flowed over to my grandmother after he died. She had to take responsibility for investments and I learnt about that from her. Because I knew right from that early age how important money was and it how can totally screw up people's brains if things go wrong financially, like it happened to my parents, by being guarantors for my brother. She was perhaps the strongest influence to show me how money works and how you can make money. So again it was nothing to do with my sexuality. It was about that overriding worry about money. If you talk to people from an ordinary working class background in Australia it was always about money.

When I was in teacher's college I had a girlfriend, and that sort of just happened, until I put my hands there and figured, 'Well, that's boobs'. Then I put my hands down there and realised there was nothing to hold on to. I was eighteen at that stage, at eighteen you want to experiment, you want to try and I thought, 'There's nothing to hold onto. What am I going to do? There's nothing to play with down there'.

I just completely lost interest. It was okay, I liked her as a person and talking to her as a person, we had plenty to talk about, but sexually that wasn't going to happen. It just didn't interest me at all. That was my experience with girls in regards to sex, not much experience, but that's the whole thing, there was nothing to hold onto, nothing to play with.

Michael

At the end of my first year of university I made my first trip to South East Asia (December 1970–February 1972). I visited Malaysia, Singapore, Indonesia and Thailand, and though I had a visa to Laos, I was later advised by the embassy not to proceed. In Indonesia I made contact with church groups, still somewhat in trauma, especially in Bali from the coup of 1965. But I also visited Hindu and Buddhist temples whose religions were also to form part of my Bachelor of Divinity degree.

For two of the three years of my degree (1970-1972) I was granted a scholarship for lay persons. I supported myself in 1970 while studying and taught Asian history to a single class of forty students and I had become a marking examiner in the subject at Adelaide High. One of my students there was from Singapore and later I had stayed with his parents and siblings in 1970, where I also I met his sister, a lawyer. I courted her until 1973 without success due to the dictates of Chinese arranged marriage, a barrier too hard to surmount.

And so I never married. I have often puzzled as to where and when I became aware of gay issues and my own sexuality. I was naively untouched by the concept of same-sex attraction at school and my first years of university. I was fifteen when I discovered masturbation and I received no sex education from my parents, though I did embrace solitary nudism early after leaving home. I remember asking my mother once after reading a newspaper about the meaning of 'carnal knowledge' and 'loitering' cited in police reports. I was told to look up a dictionary, which proved largely unhelpful. My father's friend and best man in 1941 was later charged with 'loitering'.

At university I read the works of Auden and Isherwood, as part of my history course. When I was studying Christian ethics for my BD degree, homosexuality was presented in the context of traditional conservative theology. I never thought of myself as in 'that way' at all. Its treatment of it was pretty scant, though it may have been the first time I heard of the Wolfenden report, which came out in 1965-66 in Britain, but I was not presented with any questioning of the traditional Christian prohibition on homosexuality. Euthanasia was more a preoccupation of my teacher. I was aware of the setting up in Adelaide in 1971 of a branch of the Campaign Against Moral Persecution. I think one of my fellow ministerial student candidates had some brochures. I had bought a copy of Dennis Altman's Homosexual Oppression, scarcely read. The drowning of Dr Duncan was in the newspapers. But I was more interested in focusing on my Greek to pass the exams than a lot of those issues relating to homosexuality. I was also dating a woman from the church at the time.

I am convinced that it was my Divinity degree that secured me a teaching position at an independent church school in 1973. I had lost my fundamentalism during my BD studies and having travelled overseas quite a bit, I realised that being a single missionary was never going to work for me and that teaching was what I did best. I planned to stay for a couple of years at the school with a view to getting enough money to go off to Europe to travel and work, like many friends had done. But I ended up staying much longer and travelling in my summer vacation before tying myself down with a mortgage in 1980.

Thomas

The main impacting event was when I was molested before I reached puberty by a family friend. I liked this man and felt sorry for him because he had been a prisoner of war and had lost his wife. I was questioned once by my father because I think other people were asking questions, 'has he ever touched you?' and I defended him and said 'no' thinking that they might send me to a boys home. I probably knew it was wrong but I'm the sort of person that wouldn't dob someone in because of what he'd gone through. Like I said, I knew it was wrong and I thought he had suffered enough. He's passed on now and I have moved on. I'm not like the other people who want to dredge up the past. I feel like that's happened. The experience, bringing it back is not going to change anything. I don't know what would have happened if I said 'yes' to my parents. I just got over it. A lot of people who get molested just don't get over things like that, I guess.

I just felt very sorry for him, and you know we get to those teenage years and you're experimenting sexually anyway. He did want more at one stage but I said I wasn't happy to do that and he respected that. It was only touching and stuff but one stage he put the question on me about anal penetration and I said, 'no, I'm not into that' and he didn't force it on me, to do that to me. I was really happy that he didn't sort of go any further. He was a really good family friend and my father is a doctor and he was one of his patients. They always say it's family friends that do that sort of things to people. I don't know.

I think at that stage (schooling years) I was attracted

to both sexes and I experimented with both, I actually did get married and don't regret that. I went to Tudor House, which is a junior King's School, which is a private school in Moss Vale. King's School in Sydney is one of the elite schools and I think I went through a test or something. I don't think I passed it very well so I didn't go there. I think if I had been quite smart my parents would put me through a fairly good school. I was quite happy just to go to the local high school. They were co-ed as well and growing up I was attracted to the boys and stuff like that but when I was growing up I don't think I knew of any homosexuals in the school, or if they were, they weren't out. I used to look at my dad's medical books for stuff and they didn't really tell me anything. Today you could do it (be out), but back then you had to suppress and hide stuff like that if you did have feelings for someone. You can do it these days but not in Queensland. It's still a bit of an issue.

When I was eighteen I wanted to see (gay) stuff from Sydney, but I didn't find out a lot of this until I was much older because there was no information out there. Today you just go on the Internet and it's all there, not back then. I'm meeting a lot of guys online that are actually married and we've all been suppressed and they couldn't come out when they were that age. For me, working at the bank, they probably would have fired me. You couldn't do that (come out). If someone found out, you would have lost your job back then. There's a lot of guys who got married because that's what you did then, and now I'm finding that so much, talking to these older guys my age, they just didn't do it. Now they're still married but are not happy and they can't get out of it. I said no, I'm not going to live this for the rest of my life, I need to move on.

David H

I've generally had two streams in my life: the classical music and piano in particular and also an interest in literature. I actually did a liberal arts diploma at Hartley College in Adelaide and did creative writing as a major, and got into writing back in the 70s. I did some qualifications in music and also the literature stuff, so I would identify myself as an artist if you want a specific term. I'm actually starting to work on a book myself where I'm going to bring some of the themes of my life together. So there's always been those two streams, and I have never been the sort of person who said I wanted to be a fireman and that, or a policeman or whatever. It's always been this more creative range of stuff. Out of that has come working for a singing teacher and an accompanist with the Melbourne Orchestra for several years, 20 years plus of broadcasting with public radio in Melbourne, classical music. I think the sabotaging factor in my career, in a lot of ways, was that I've had a lot of ill health since I was about eighteen, which I've had to work on and I'm dealing with multiple conditions now that are not that easy to live with. If I didn't have such strong willpower it would be a lot harder. One of them is a thing called FMS (fibromyalgia syndrome), which is a weird malfunction in the pain system. So I get a lot of muscle pain, spasms and other things going on, and even playing piano is not a physically comfortable thing to do, so I have to program myself. When I do concerts like a did in May, the year before I literally have to go to training, to train to what it's like.

It's very interesting going through that process of peeling the layers back. While I was floundering around a lot of the time I learned about who I was and what I wanted through some relationships I made. The other thing I've had to deal with is very poor self-image, which may not appear as I'm talking to you now, but through that early background my sense of self was pretty appalling. I was appallingly shy and when the sexuality thing came up and I recognised what it was, it also just pinched, because that was not a good thing to be so I had to work through that as well. Now I'm fine with it, and luckily—even though my father was a lapsed Catholic—I didn't have the horrible Catholic thing to deal with. I think in the past, Catholicism particularly has almost destroyed a lot of gay men because of the way they were taught about their sexuality. So I'm happy with where I am now as an artist, but I do find Australia a very frustrating place to live, because when it comes to sport we will pour any amount of money, any amount of energy, any amount of enthusiasm into it, but the poor old arts are on the other side and needs to be brought back into balance. Though I don't quite know how to do that. I think a lot of artists in Australia would find the same thing, it is frustrating.

I had a breakdown when I was in my twenties, and looking back I think that was part of the process of being very repressed and going inside rather than taking my sister's approach, which was to just rebel and fight against whatever it was. I put all that pressure on myself and I remember at one point I was on antidepressants, which in those days really made a complete zombie out of you. Eventually I decided I was going to stop those and just get on with it, which I did. I went back to piano study and went up through the piano grades and did a diploma in music. On my first go at a university degree, because I had too much to sort out, I just fell in a crashing heap. When I went to Hartley in Adelaide I was about thirty-three. I started again and got on with it and I was very good at it. I went through some of the stuff that I wrote recently and thought I'm impressed with that.

Hugh

Now, even though Dr Duncan was murdered in 1972 the actual decriminalisation law took three years to come through. But still for me South Australia looked like the promised land. A job came up here, and I jumped at it. It meant actually a lower salary but I was willing to accept the drop in income to get here. My new job was with the ABC Adelaide Singers. That only lasted a year, then I went back to being an education producer again. It was an exciting time to be in Adelaide. The activists were out in force, to move towards decriminalisation, so I wrote to my local state member.

For the first year I was here, in 1975, I stayed with various people. I shared a flat with another gay guy. I was not having sex with him. He went out one night to Veale Gardens, the notorious Veale Gardens, and came back with blood all over his face and the side of his car kicked in. He went to the police about it but nothing much happened. I mean, they were quite sympathetic, they didn't say, 'You're a poofter, what do you expect to happen?' They took details and I guess followed up as well as they could, but the guys had left long before they got there.

That was a bit shocking and as soon as I could I moved, in 1975, into a long-term gay relationship. It wasn't with Philip. It was with somebody else who was sort of a bit like I had been before I went to the psychiatrist. He was consumed with guilt, he was a strong Lutheran and he had almost no sense of humour. I knew deep down that it was not a good match, but I really wanted to have a long-term relationship with another man, so I was prepared to put up with it. The sex was not particularly good, but we sort of rubbed along, especially to start with. He was looking for someone too. It just sort of declined, it got worse and worse. He used to go and have dinner with his Lutheran family every night, so I'd eat in the ABC canteen. I was producing two series of programs, one of music for schools and the other of German language. We sort of drifted further and further apart, not in a sexual way, just through not having similar interests or attitudes. Things came to a bit of a head when we were invited to a dinner party with a couple of other gay guys and their friends, and he took violent exception to something that somebody had said and stalked out of the place. It was extremely, extremely uncomfortable. I knew then that things were not going well.

I still supported him when he had his big birthday party. I chipped in and helped him pay part of it, for the wine and so on, but the relationship didn't really ever work properly. Eventually he realised that too and he said to me, 'I don't love you anymore, we'll have to go our separate ways'. In a way that hurt, because after nine years it was quite a shock, but at the same time it was the best thing he could have done for me, again it set me free.

Michael

On reflection my best personal achievement was the early investment I made in education and travel as a vehicle for new learning, seizing opportunities not available to my parents. After my disappointment with my first year of university in 1961, I persevered, fortified by hard won study skills and self-discipline. I probably got more out of my Bachelor of Divinity course through critical analysis, but my education has given me a lifelong commitment to continuous learning.

I resumed overseas travel in 1973 as additional investment in my future rather than material consolidation, attending opera performances in New York, London, Vienna and Paris, and exploring historical sites and galleries. After some twenty years (1986-2005) married to a mortgage, I resumed overseas travel with a focus on central Asia and China.

I eventually, if perhaps belatedly, made an investment in property. I had focussed on travel in my younger years rather than getting a roof over my head. I recall my deputy headmaster took me aside one day saying 'right you've done a lot of travelling, now it's time to buy a house' and he was right. I did that, but it also meant that I wasn't able to travel at leisure and I learnt to live more frugally.

David D

I found it difficult at first to be open about my sexuality. I was bisexual and nearly married three times. I had a major breakdown at age twenty-four in 1974 and was diagnosed with schizophrenia (Later in life at age fifty-two 2001 I was diagnosed as bipolar). During my hospitalisation at Larundel I was referred to a psychiatrist who supposedly was going to cure me of my homosexuality. He got me to fill out a question-and-answer form in front of him.

It was very fashionable for psychiatrists to cure people of their homosexuality, well to go through the motions because it was illegal still to be a homosexual and I think that the mental health authorities thought it was obligatory to get people out of their bad habits, and it was regarded as a habit rather than a way of life. I was blabbering on to everyone including my partner Marilyn and my dad and my sisters how I was involved in bisexuality and so I got the psychiatrist who was going to cure me. But he was smart, he knew that he had a job to do but he also knew that really it was a ruse. A week later he said to me I needed to be more honest with myself and not fight it. He was really helping people and saying to them 'David don't fight it just be honest with yourself' and that was a really curing me. He had a duplicity role. I was more open with my second and third female partners because of that.

My first love was when I was twenty-one, maybe twenty-two. I met Marilyn on the dance floor at the Melbourne Town Hall when she was seventeen, very beautiful. We had a very passionate relationship. We got involved with going to the drive-in in my EH sedan and making passionate love more than watching the movies. I thought this could be good—this marriage business—but I was still feeling troubled by my attraction to gay men at the same time as being with Marilyn. There was guilt and there was confusion; it was difficult, enjoyable but difficult. When I was thirteen, I think I was coming out of the Olympic pool from swimming training, had taken off my wet speedos and just put a tracksuit on, and this man was in a car outside the Olympic pool with a South Australian rego and was pretending to be confused about where he was. He had a map in front of him and he beckoned me into the car and started feeling me up.

That was probably my first sexual experience, but very close to that there were the St Kilda Sea Baths, which were amazing. They were traditional English-type baths with a quadrant with parallel piers and a pier at the end so it's closed from the sea. In those piers were sunbathing rooms where men would all be sunbathing in the nude and having a bit of fun with one another. I was thirteen and I would stand on the edge of the pier looking into the baths with my back to the sunbathing area. I had this pair of speedos on but this middle-aged man probably in his fifties got behind me and started rubbing his leg against my bum. That led to my first intercourse experience.

I got involved with a young man who was studying in the Anglican priest ministry at the Malvern Squash Way, which was quite a posh squash centre with an indoor pool. He had these jockettes on, they were amazing in the shower. I later went to visit him at Queens College, Melbourne University and we had fun there. He had a motorbike and sometimes I rode on the back of the motorbike with him. Initially we went to backyards and that went on for a few years. He said initially that I was very introverted but later he could see me developing a bit in my analytical thinking and was really pleased that I was getting out of my introversion.

While I worked for fifteen years with Trustees Executors and ANZ Trustees from 1974 to 1989 doing wills and estates, I saw a lot of human nature in my work. My clients told me I had a good bedside manner, which I thought was a great compliment and I'm a pretty good listener. I initially did my articles, which was an article clerk's course for four years, not just one like the university. I had a breakdown in 1974 with my work-related problems, possibly combined with sexuality, and I had a breakdown. I thought that litigation and general law was going to be too much for my constitution. Dad noticed an advertisement for a probate officer with Trustees Executors and we thought wills and estates were a bit more laid back than litigation and family law and all that, so I got the job with Trustees Executors and absolutely loved it. Despite more breakdowns and that, I still loved it.

Later, actually in 1986, I was offered to manage ANZ Trustees in Darwin and thought this would be nice as there were so many perks to the job. They gave me a two-year contract to work in Darwin in 1987 and 1988. So I moved up there. I had not long bought a house in South Melbourne and dad's second marriage had broken up fairly quickly, so I asked dad to live in my South Melbourne house and pay me a modest rental while I lived up in Darwin with my two year contract. That's what happened but during those two years I started on marijuana, which stuffed up my mental health. It's easy to be wise in hindsight. When I became ill because of the marijuana about mid-1988, dad came up. Actually I went back to Melbourne to enable me to see psychiatrists and become superannuated. We went back to Darwin after being hospitalised for a while and decided to live together. We went back to Darwin because as we thought it would be a great place to retire. This was to last ten years . My brother-in-law, David, called us the odd couple. Dad went a bit anti-gay when he was first living with me, he told a lot of my gay friends to piss off on the phone and that was rather upsetting and isolating. I just steered a different course in my life and became involved in the Labor Party in Darwin as well as Red Cross and the Uniting Church Nightcliff op shop.

So not having a lot of gay friends but still having a few, and dad was still accepting of my few remaining friends, I got involved with the Labor Party in Darwin. We both did a lot of work for them and met people like Gough Whitlam, Joan Kirner and Paul Keating. We were very much loved by the Labor Party and we did a lot of work for Red Cross, including the library trolley at the hospital, and I ran an op shop for the Nightcliff Uniting Church for eight years up there. Absolutely loved it.

Travis

I think identity is actually a problematic thing. It is easy to use premade labels. So maybe I'll start with the ready-made labels and identify as a gay man. It is what it is for me now. I had a really, really common experience. I had this period of time of being so-called bisexual and I can relate the moment when that changed. At school how did I identify? As a young person, I wouldn't have identified myself by sexuality, bearing in mind homosexuality was illegal for most of my school years and became legal in South Australia in 1975, when I was in year twelve. The legal message, and all the subtle messages, were that being gay is an aberration, it's not an option.

So, how did I identify myself? Academic, studious, high-achieving, family person aiming for a successful professional career and lovely wife and four children.

That was the case until I became very close to marrying into one family, and then I thought it's problematic when you find a girlfriend's brother more interesting. I still don't quite know how that happened, how that all fell apart, because I think the usual trajectory at that time was that if you had managed to achieve that kind of front you'd go for it. It just never occurred to me that I would actually be able to live that sort of lie. So in my mid-twenties I threw that family idea out the window, so I'm not sure what I did with identity then.

Really, I didn't want to cause the hurt and disappointment that would be necessary and I think I did think 'if I don't do the hurt and disappointment now it's only going to be worse later on, so best start'. I still did it rather passively, I wasn't at all upfront or forthright, but the objective was achieved. She went and married a lawyer and I went to their wedding. We danced at her wedding and I felt very, very awkward when she told me I was still the number one choice. I haven't seen her since, but she found out when she asked a mutual friend sometime later and asked how I am, whether I had a nice girlfriend and got told I had a nice boyfriend. I didn't get a congratulations from her but I hoped it put it in context for her, hopefully she is grateful at the bullet dodged.

I was certainly not involved in protesting. I was terribly, terribly closeted. I didn't come out to my family and everyone until my early thirties, which was in the early nineties. I wasn't involved in this sort of overt protest movement, but I was involved in individual interventions dealing with the treatment of us, by the police in particular. I remember in the early seventies the death of Dr Duncan when he was thrown into the Torrens in Adelaide. That did have an impact on me because I did understand that that's potentially me and I did understand that the police were not our friends.

Anxiety saved my life. I was at school in the seventies, I went from school to university in the late seventies, early eighties. I was chock-full of anxieties about my friends and family, and academic performance, and how I was going in University, and relationships, and particularly around sexuality. And so my sexual explorations were very constrained by anxiety and fear. Long story short, if my sexual exploration hadn't been constrained by fear about trivial things like catching syphilis or somebody finding out or anything like that, then likely I'd have died of HIV a long time ago. The late seventies was the period of time when gay men were busily getting infected with HIV at a time when nobody had any idea what it was or that it even existed. This happened to a lot of people; that they thought the only consequence is going to be maybe needing a penicillin injection once or twice a year, and with no thought that it's more serious than that, and I certainly didn't know any better than anyone else. I was just at the time quite inhibited and therefore very lucky.

David H

It was just before I came over to Adelaide that homosexuality was decriminalised, but I remember visiting someone who I got to know and we were in bed and afterwards I thought 'oh that was my first legal fuck'. It didn't feel any different to any other one, because it wouldn't anyway, and I remember thinking that. The lights didn't shine down or a giant voice boom out or anything like that it was just the usual.

Because of my self-image it's been very difficult to work through my identity. This actually shocks me looking back from 2017, but I can remember thinking that if I'm sexually active when I'm twenty-one (obviously these feelings were there before that), then it will be all right, and that seems utterly insane to me now. I mean what difference does that make anyway, but somehow I had a real battle with coming to terms with being gay, and it was probably not until around the age of thirty that I became really comfortable with it. Now it's just second nature. Through that long period starting from about twenty-one, I'd quite often have periods of counselling with various people like university counsellors and things like that and I remember there was a gent called Dennis at Melbourne University and I used to go to chat to him. He was gay and came out later in life, he died last year I think. I suppose it was talking with people like that who were okay with themselves and obviously older than me. If the subject came up that was no big deal for them, they will just talk very naturally about it. So he had an effect in his own way, that's quite a while back now. Most of it I've done myself really. I'm really racking my brain to think anybody who was a major influence.

David D

My second encounter with marriage was with my secretary, Jan. I bumped into her in Rome where she was on a Trafalgar Tour and I had been to see my sister, Dorothy. I was at an historical venue, and I saw her there. I said there was a European Cup final on tomorrow night and would she like to go to it. She said yes, and that was the start of a romance. I had explained to her about my bisexuality and I thought everything was fine, not really knowing whether I could have the marriage and still have gay men friends, but hoping that way. When we went back to Melbourne we started a relationship and decided to get married. That's when mum came along giving me advice and dad protecting me and Jan deciding that the marriage wasn't going ahead, it was five days before the marriage.

There had been a work collection for a marriage gift for us, but when she broke up and before she went off to Sydney she told everyone in the office that I was gay. I became the butt of jokes and jibes in the very conservative company I was working for. My politics were never revealed. That was 1977. Actually I had a wonderful boss who was protective of my mental breakdown. I had a breakdown not long after it fell through with Jan. My boss was very good. We had disability insurance and he said you can do some menial jobs for a while such as checking rate notices. Trustees Executors was one of the very old-fashioned companies where you had a job for life. We had a ninety-five-year-old auditor. It was a wonderful feeling that you had that security and that you could borrow money from the company at three percent for a house and they lent me $58,000 on an $80,000 house. At three percent, payable over forty years. These were the years when home loan interest rates rose to sixteen percent. The company was one of the first with superannuation for women. They were marvellous.

By that stage I wasn't getting bullied so much, although with the jibes and the jokes after Jan let loose it was a bit difficult and they were singing out hello sailor songs and 'Poof the Magic Dragon' and all that sort of stuff. I had an offsider who was very lazy. He came from a wealthy legal firm and they had given him a job because of his connections with our money market. He was hopeless. He was on the grog all the time. He would not do much work and I was saddled with supervising him and he was introducing me to all his friends as a bachelor gay and all this business. I tried to get him sacked but it didn't succeed. That was about the time the company went broke, changing to ANZ Trustees as part of the ANZ Bank.

The third attempt at marriage was the best of the lot because she was my sister Dorothy's partner in the haute couture business at the Canberra Brickworks, and she decided to move to Mount Martha to be near her brother. She had a daughter with cerebral palsy who was nine. Dorothy asked if I would do the conveyancing for her shift to Mount Martha, which I did. On the day of the settlement I got the keys and went down to Mount Martha to give them to her. When I was doing this I was the recipient of a very lovely kiss and that was the start of the wonderful relationship. Before we bought a house together I had been in a beautiful house in Toorak (just off the Toorak village) with a wonderful gay lifestyle. I thought that living together was going to be sensational. She was stunning in her looks and vivacious and beautiful with her clothes. She was a friend of John Gordon and she had organised to have a fellow masseur with a Canberra rugby team who she knew was bisexual to come down and have a threesome with us. Unfortunately we broke up before it was to occur.

My first homosexual live-in relationship was with Nigel from 1979 to about 1983. Dad was against Nigel. I would go and have dinner at Mum and Dad's. My house in Glen Iris was about four kilometres from theirs, but I was frequenting them a lot. Dad would drive me back and on one occasion Nigel was there waiting in the street and Dad was absolutely infuriated. I wasn't particularly well and Dad thought that he would muck up my health. Nigel lived in an Edwardian mansion in St Kilda. I decided to move in with him and sell my house in Glen Iris. The day I sold my house and the contract signed for the sale, he said 'oh mum has decided that I'm not to sell you half of my house', as he had promised. So I went to live with him I had all this money in the term deposit from the sale of my house and I thought that this relationship is not going marvellously. He'd wake up in the middle of the night and start pulling at my hair, tearing my hair and saying 'you fucking bastard' and this sort of thing. I thought, 'no, this is no good' so after about six months of abuse I moved out and bought the house in Toorak.

Gabby

I left home at fifteen and a half and went and lived in town because my father had a rule 'what you do in my house is my rules, if you want to do anything else, leave'. You might want to come back but do it elsewhere, and that's what I did. I went off and ventured into town I went into community improvement for youth in the city which was helping socially disadvantaged mentally retarded people go on camps and being support parent workers for them and then that grew off into nightclubs. So I got to meet lots and lots of people and started to meet the seedy side of Adelaide. At sixteen years of age

I was meeting people like detectives in Victoria Square and many going along and meeting of the baddies because Victoria Square, twelve o'clock, two o'clock in the morning you have the nastiest of all people walking about. That got me into nightclub life.

I had battled hiding my transgender in my teens. I battled it very hard because I worked in an industry which did not, well the people I associated with in my teens and young adult life would not have accepted me doing that. They were not of nice character or nice people. I struggled watching at sixteen years of age other transgender women get beaten up and harassed and was unable to do anything as soon as sixteen or seventeen-year-old boy. Because you've got these great big huge monsters of men with tattoos and were bikers.

At that time I was also very experimental with life. I mean I was experimenting with drugs and alcohol, lots of alcohol. I worked in a nightclub, a strip club nightclub, and I was the assistant manager by the time I was eighteen. I was charged under the liquor licensing act, that's at sixteen and a half, for overcrowding of a nightclub on North Terrace and it was also a nightclub which I saved two hundred and fifty people's lives one night because a fire was upstairs and I went down and got them all out. My teenage years was a mixed bag because I was dealing with being transgender but I was supplementing it by mixing with the gay world. My only way I could deal was being and getting my feminine fix to keep me going in a sense was either that covert time when I was able to lock up the door and I was able to pull out a few clothes from a bag I might've had or I might have gone to the sauna and get laid anything like that. At sixteen, seventeen you'd be, probably in a gay club, might get taken off by an old boy by the name of Big B or Wally or Max might take you off to his house in the eastern suburbs. I mixed with a lot, a lot of people of very different varieties.

I was out, the community was out, it wasn't hidden because you had Penthouse nightclub, you had the place on Hindley Street up near, below the Apollo apartment, you had Patches and Q nightclub that went for many eras as a place where I was working from. That site offered playboy and playgirl and was very upmarket at the time it had a lot of gay influence in there because they were probably the only two clubs to open after one o'clock in the morning, two o'clock in the morning was Patches nightclub and the Mars Bar. So it would be like a rotating cycle between people going to the Mars Bar and Patches and so on because they were the late night venues at those times. You'd have a mixture because as being strip club you'd have your very brilliant transgender strippers, I mean they were just brilliant. This one named Kerry, she was immaculate. There were transgender women out there but it wasn't a hundred percent safe. They could go out and walk but it was really safe for them. I remember being terrified at, I think it was probably about sixteen and a half, seventeen, and I watched two getting beaten up by these guys in Hindley

Street. I remember watching two girls, watching one's silicone tit being pushed right around her side. Those things, they leave an impression, do you wannabe on the receiving end? I mean I'm watching this happen and I'm dealing with my own issues inside knowing that, that's me, that's me, I'm that person, I'm that girl. I'm dealing with what she is dealing with but she's got guts to do something that I wanted to do, I needed to do. She's doing it but she is copping all this harassment and beaten up.

Mahamati

I think that sort of wafted by me (homosexuality decriminalisation). I think I was caught up in my own little world at that time, which was being married, I was working office type jobs, and David was teaching, I was fairly involved with everything he did in a school sense and we had Barb. When I look back at other things in those years we had kids from St Mary's, we also looked after some kids from what was Glandore Boys Home in those days, which was a bit harsher. Some kids were there on remand and some were there because their parents weren't available or in jail and you know, kids were sort of stranded for a period of time in sort of state care instead of church care, which seemed to be a bit more caring.

Barb we adopted and then shortly after that and I'm not quite sure what happened when I look back on it. David had applied to be principal at a small school on Aboriginal lands, so we went bush for three years to Nepabunna up near Arkaroola. Barb was what we thought was the only white kid at school, all the other kids were Aboriginal at Nepabunna, and I had two more kids while we were there, Tony and Megan. I was still very much involved with school and in school life. Friendships with Aboriginal women and kids, very close friendship with one of the infant teachers who had applied for a job, she had just come back from being in India and she was sort a bit lost in that the guy she wanted to marry wasn't allowed to be married because of the caste and all of the caste issues that I knew nothing about, I knew absolutely zilch. So I got to engage with her from that experience from India and her travel which started me on India, putting that in the back of my mind. She'd go away for the school holidays and come back with wonderful spices and she'd make curry out of kangaroo tail and lots of things. I thought that was incredibly exotic.

It (Nepabunna) was one of the first schools that were relinquished under the United Aborigines Mission for the Education Department to run the school. Previously to that missionaries were there and they taught. By all accounts they did a good job and certainly did a lot for the people but also stamped out the culture. Kids were discouraged from using their own language and it was very Baptist in its church origin. The men were often away during the week working on cattle farms and sheep stations in the area, all the sort of work they could get and would often be back at Nepabunna on the weekends so very often during the week it was only the older men and younger boys who went to school up to year eight they taught them and if they wanted to go on they did boarding at Leigh Creek or Port Augusta where they had relatives.

We sort of played along to some extent. We respected the rules. There was no alcohol on the reserve and they used to do atrocious things. They'd stop the cars and search people's cars before they came in to make sure the Aboriginal people hadn't bought alcohol. Those sorts of things, looking back at them, were absolutely atrocious infringements and I felt, we both felt, back then that we abided by their rules. They were quite a bit older than us, we respected the work they did do. They used to do flying doctor clinics every morning, people would come up with the radio and Mrs Halliday was quite an accomplished bush nurse and saved a lot of people's health and lives but there was a cost, which was certainly the cost of the culture. Now I think there are several of the lads we were involved with and David taught are the elders who get quoted all the time and they run a great eco centre and it's very interesting. Barb has always had a very strong friendship and affinity with them, she still goes back a couple of times a year.

There was a family, a white family who lived in one of

the stations near to us. Sort of as people do in the bush, we look to make friends with people, station owners or workers on stations. The kids had mutual play stuff together with kids around the same age. Barb would always go places and would usually bring some friends. One particular one was Sharon, and I remember one of the first times we went to the station and she started to walk around the back door. I asked where she was going and she said we never go to the front door and that's changing. So they have a rule that we didn't even know existed until we saw them play out like that. It is just how it was. People who were in charge of those sorts of stations were not mean or horrible it was how their parents were and what they did. They had good fair work conditions and all those sorts of things for people but certainly when we bring Barb would also friends with her people would wonder about this. It was considered unusual. We'd take them into Leigh Creek at different times bunch of kids and then bring them back to Adelaide on different holidays and stay at my mother's and other places, David's parents' as well on school holidays. I think people thought it was a different time I guess that people on those stations, they certainly have different attitudes and rules that weren't written down but different expectations with the aboriginal people and the white people.

That felt odd to be seen as privileged. I guess it was an encounter with finding out what white privilege was before I really had those words for it. It probably never entered my head at that age. You know I knew people more affluent and who could afford things like cars, private schools and stuff like that. We didn't, so I didn't really feel privileged. We were never very rich, that was for sure. My father was just working in the factory and bands. So it was never that easy but when I look back at it having been sent to high school having absolutely no idea how they afforded the costs that it must have been. You know, having got a granddaughter at the moment who was at high school two years ago, oh god what a cost, and living with a single father. I don't know how they did it. Those sorts of things just weren't questioned, they just did it. It was never much conversation about it. I couldn't get a bike because we couldn't afford it, that was expected. I had no idea how much other things would have cost. I didn't actually feel privileged. I saw kids richer and better off.

During the time at Glencoe, I guess it was first through Prue this teacher who is up at Nepabunna with us and her connections and stuff and somehow got involved with India and as soon as I went to work for a year and had a sort of money I could save up I left over I went off to India after several weeks during school holidays. In the time got involved with an orphanage a few things like that down south at the very tip of India and through that we began sponsoring kids and encouraging other people to sponsor kids and set up sewing centres so these nuns would get money from fundraised money and they set up a bit more formal learning centres, sewing centres in the orphanages for kids who couldn't afford to go on to high school. So they would have their sewing machine and that make stuff like blouses and stuff like that and having informal schooling along the way they would read and they'd sing and they'd read the newspaper and have the radio and bits and pieces. That involved me going a couple of times and refreshing photos for sponsoring stuff and then David and I took the kids to India for five months in a period as well. A bit later took the kids and it had a major effect on them. Barb, the eldest didn't go she was pretty established in Adelaide with a job and didn't want to leave and didn't see it is a great adventure but the younger kids did so we went to India then when Paul was five and the others were eleven and twelve. We had five months in India and spent time in orphanages and convents that was why we're still married and before the chunk of time at Rape Crisis and going back to school and having relationships and leaving.

David H

When I was going through my archives recently from forty years ago and me being arrested in the street march as I will explain. I look back and thought do we still need to have those homosexual conferences although I believe they're still going on, because things have changed in so many ways like the fact that same-sex marriage will eventually come up to be dealt with and we are having the referendum or the postal whatever the fuck it is which enrages me and a lot of other people. So to go backwards going to the conference and I was talking to somebody about it and who is writing a book on Mardi Gras recently and I said to him I think it was set up in some ways because what I remember was it was a Sunday afternoon, there was a proposal to have a street march from Paddington down to Taylor Square and some of the organisers of the conference said don't do it you will be arrested. That there was a body of people in the audience saying no, no, no it will be fine, we will walk on the footpath it's not illegal procession because we're not on the road so being naive South Australian because I was at Hartley and the student union had paid for two or three of us to go and we took off down the footpath and as we got down to Taylor Square and the road sort of funnels down the police had all the side streets blocked off and they were around the corners, not visible and as we got into the focal point a guy with a megaphone came out and said you've got thirty seconds to disperse or whatever it was and as we turn around to leave they just pounced on people and started arresting them. We were all charged and the names of the arrested were published on the front page of the *Sydney Morning Herald* including teachers and whatever and I got to the papermail back in Adelaide because my address wasn't put on it. The cases came up the first one pleaded guilty because he was going overseas and wanted to finalise it. The rest of us ended up in a joint thing and the charges were eventually dropped but it took quite some time.

I can't remember the numbers now, I thought it was about sixty but I might be wrong. Eventually the charges were dropped but we were photographed getting in the police van, but when I couriered later to say to have those destroyed they said no photos were taken so whether it was ASIO or whoever, who knows. I wrote to Neville Wran who later became or might be the Premier then but he was also the Police Minister saying what had happened. Don Dunstan was my local member, the Premier of South Australia and I wrote to him and I recently found those letters and got a reply back. Officially the Labor Party in South Australia wasn't allowed to criticise the Labor Party in New South Wales, I remember someone saying, and this was the period when New South Wales was really very corrupt and homosexuality was still illegal I think. Things were on the cusp of changing I think maybe at the conference there was a body who really wanted to push the boundaries and we sort of got stuck into the middle of that. It was quite an experience because we were in the lock-up all day long and we were trying to raise bail money there was some telephone problem with Adelaide to get the money through. I remember that took a long time to actually get out there and luckily I didn't need to go back to Sydney later on to appear because it was eventually dropped. Somebody was the liaison for me and I used to write to him and find out what was going on. So they were some of the papers are found recently to go onto the guy who is writing a book about it. I've never been to the Mardi Gras I think next year's the fortieth anniversary of all that and I'm entitled right on the bus I believe because of the arrest so I should really try and do that.

I nearly knocked him (Dunstan) down in the art gallery one day. I was coming in through the back door and he was coming the other way and he was really quite a short little guy and we just sort smiled at each other and I went first I think. I didn't have a lot to do with him. He was a very significant force for changing anti-gay laws and things like that in Adelaide in South Australia and such a breath of fresh air and such a shock to the Conservatives when he got into office, including going into Parliament one day in his pink shorts.

Philip

Once, when was a kid I tried going to church, but it wasn't ever really interesting to me about Christianity. But later in my life I became a Buddhist monk, and that was deeply satisfying, because it gave me that opportunity of living with other men, but not in competition with other men, not like it was in the Army, or a sports team. It was working together in harmony with other men and that was really, really satisfying. It put in my mind the idea that men can live together and they can live cooperatively, and they can work together towards goals. Whereas a lot of things in our society are saying that men have to be in some sort of competition, someone has to come out on top, and someone has to be better than the other one.

Being a Buddhist monk was really good and I enjoyed that a lot, but at about twenty-five, twenty-six years old I realised, 'Okay, am I going to continue doing this in Thailand or am I going to go back to Australia and make some money?' And I knew already what my answer was. What I wanted to do was make money. So it was back to Australia.

I worked as an interpreter, that was hourly paid. At that time I was finishing the university course that I'd disrupted to go and live in Thailand. I was also taking care of the Temple, the Buddhist Temple, so I didn't have any costs to pay whilst I was studying at university. Back then it was that lucky era that there was plenty of money in Australia and university was free. It's unbelievable when I say that now, but university was free. And because I was taking care of the Temple I had free accommodation and free food, but I was also working as an interpreter at the hospital. What's ironic about that is that it was mostly to do with the ante-natal clinic so, actually, I know more about the sexual reproduction of women than most straight men, even though I've never gone there myself.

It's actually been pretty easy. I've been very focused on how much did I get paid per hour at work and that's really annoyed a lot of people. That's perhaps the biggest annoyance that people had with me at work, that I was so focused on how much money am I going to make for doing this, how obvious I was about it and how upfront I was about it: how much my time is worth. Whereas they were into talking about commitment to the organisation and making statements about the organisation, about what the organisation stands for and so on. I was just really interested in how much money I could make per hour and how many hours I'm going to be teaching and what I'm going to do that money, buying shares. That was the biggest sticking points between myself and some of the other people at work. It wasn't anything to do with being gay, it was that in-your-face attitude I have of how much money am I going to make for my time, and this is what I'm going to do with my money: I'm going to buy such and such shares. Whereas many of the other people at the workplace were highly unionised. They'd started some years before me and so they were tenured and they believed in the organisation, whereas I had no belief in the organisation. So there was a very big ideological difference there, that I believed in the money I was getting, in what I was going to do with it; whereas they believed in the organisation and they believed the organisation was going to go on giving them what they needed.

1980s

The HIV/AIDS Epidemic
First official diagnoses of HIV/Aids was in 1982. There were many suspected cases of HIV in decades prior to this but it wasn't until this year that the US started to formally track the disease.[13] In June of that year the disease was referred to as Gay-Related Immune Deficiency or GRID but by September the CDC called it AIDS.[14] It took a few years before the HIV virus could be formally identified and over that period the disease was discovered amongst heterosexual partners. Despite these facts HIV was more readily found in men who have sex with men and public campaigns such as the infamous Grim Reaper fear advertisement resulted in the gay community, injecting drug users and sex workers being ostracised.

SA's Equal Opportunity Act Changed
South Australia introduced their Equal Opportunity Act 1984, which made it illegal for people to discriminate against someone on the basis of their gender identity or sexuality.[15] Within the legislation there are still some components that make it legal for religious

organisations to discriminate but most other areas are covered by this act. This meant that people could no longer be fired due to their sexuality or gender identity and secured employment for many people, particularly in conservative, non-religious businesses. It wasn't until 1988 that the federal Equal Opportunity Act was changed to match South Australia and provide security for LGBTIQ people in all jurisdictions. Prior to that change it was still legal to discriminate against LGBTIQ people in certain states and territories.

Michael

I had had my first same-sex experience quite willingly, when I was twenty in 1964, my final year at university. I was seduced by a lady hairdresser in his late twenties, both of us living in the same boarding house. But as a result of the guilt and the secrecy I remained celibate until I was thirty-eight. I know it seems silly now, but that's how it was. I never found that difficult. I was a workaholic and able to sublimate my erotic desires. Change came in mid-career when I was just forty, during my first tranche of long service leave, I took myself off to Cambridge University for nearly six months in 1984 where I was deemed a 'visiting scholar' to the History and Divinity Faculties. I have a scholarly bent and developed the routine of selected morning lectures and seminars delivered by some of the scholars whose books I had read with winter afternoons in the University Library.

I started attending a men's gay group at Cambridge, the town, not at the University, and I made some friends and one of whom was Jewish, I still keep in touch, who became a fellow traveller in France and lover. I had become sexually active in 1982 in Adelaide having reached a stage where I just hungered for physical male intimacy.

I connected with the Gay Christian Group run by an Anglican priest in London, and attended its occasional meetings. 1984 was when the nature of the AIDS crisis was starting to be better known, so I was reading more about it in journals in Cambridge and also about 'gay liberation' advocacy.

This was in some ways my 'coming out'. One of my closest Adelaide straight friends, was living in Oxford on scholarship and then working at Cambridge when I was there I came out to him. He and his wife were very supportive.

It was easy to return to teaching in Adelaide enriched by my experiences. I had travelled quite a lot to France because I had a friend in Paris. Gay friends had instilled in me that being gay was normal and they were great role models for living a fulfilling and authentic lives. I had gone to Israel as well during that time for a couple of weeks in April 1984. I've always taken an interest in Israel. It was marketed as a pilgrimage, and visited many of the holy sites and up to the Golan Heights. But then I had to come return to Adelaide.

Until 1982, in addition to a heavy teaching load, I also had responsibilities in the school's boarding house supervising some sixty boys where it was difficult to sustain a private social life. When I returned from long service leave in 1984 the headmaster was giving lectures to senior boys on what he deemed as 'aberrant sex' in light of the AIDS crisis. His predecessor wouldn't even allow any information on drugs or alcohol abuse to be directed at the boys. It was the age of the Grim Reaper and fear and denigration of homosexuality was promoted with a degree of bigotry directed at its mainly male practitioners. In the late 1980s my then partner and I shared a house. We were both busy professional guys and we socialised with a small circle of gay friends. We had been introduced by a mutual friend, becoming friends before we became lovers. We separated in the early 1990s but have remained good friends.

Non-discrimination in employment of gay teachers didn't apply to independent schools. I never felt insecure I just believed in being discreet. By the late 1990s elements of homophobia seemed to be less strident amongst boys but not always parents.

Travis

I did have a couple of interesting interactions with the police particularly around beats. Beats in the eighties in particular were certainly places to pick up and have sex but also social spaces and I think a lot of people got their social outlet about who they are at beats and I actually made some good friends there and actually had some really nice conversations. There was perhaps this comradery, this edginess around police presence and police entrapment. I had an episode in the late eighties, I was at a beat during the day met a nice guy we went to an a secluded place and we were talking and we were talking and then out of nowhere came two plainclothes police officers who were obviously very disappointed to see the two of us clothed about two metres apart and so they couldn't do us for anything decent so they proceeded to charge us for being in a restricted area on the beach. Now, as part of a university project at the time I actually knew that was not the case, I knew exactly what government departments were in control of this part of the beach and I was sure I was legally fully entitled to be there. I said, 'I don't understand that this is restricted, this is not restricted as far as I'm aware', and the police said, 'it's just been declared restricted'. The police took our names and addresses in each other's hearing and that was that. I said to this guy 'I guess we know this we know this much about each other do you want to come back to my place?', it was a good day.

Then a summons turned up at work. I told them where I worked and I think possibly I didn't need to, I didn't know that so got a summons at work, and thought that this is designed to create the most impact. I can tell you the exact year must've been 1988. The summons didn't mention sexuality it was just about being in a place where I wasn't allowed to be. I think the expectation there was that they just cause maximum embarrassments, I plead guilty, I'd be fined and I thought typical of me, that's not good enough for me. I've done nothing wrong and I'm going to wear this so I went to see a lawyer and told her my interpretation of the Coast Protection Act she looked it up, wrote back to me said, 'you're absolutely correct'. She went to court for me and had the charges dismissed. I'm uncertain most of the men who had been found in that situation would not have been in a situation to fight that and they would have taken the path of least resistance and kept it as quiet as possible.

I guess I perceive the homophobia to be overt because when it came up for discussion that perhaps homosexuality was okay the opposing voices had to actually state 'no it's not okay'. Whereas in a previous time it didn't have to be stated, so yeah, I think it was, I was subjected to being actively told that who you are is not acceptable, with a visible counterargument 'that might not be true, you are acceptable'. The topic was up for discussion but I certainly didn't have a gay identity at that stage and I think didn't really think the discussion was that relevant to me because I was going to get married and have four kids. So what affect did it have for me? Nothing I dismissed it. I didn't have a sense of this is my life you're talking about and I deflected that.

Hugh

I looked around and found this place. I had just enough saved for a deposit and was able, through the second bank I approached, to get a mortgage. At roughly the same time I met Philip through the gay bushwalking group, which was wonderful. It was like coming home, it was so free and open and it felt right and natural and

I was just so much in love with him. I thought he was the most marvellous man I'd ever seen. I used to ring him every night for about an hour and then we'd talk. He knew that I'd bought this place.

The first night of moving here was horrific, because I'm not clever with details especially practical details. I had forgotten to get the electricity put on or the phone. I had a little bit of food but not much and the place was in darkness, there was only the most basic furniture from my old place. To save money, because I didn't have much money in those days, I hired a self-drive taxi truck and got another friend to help me cart the furniture in, so I was exhausted. There were boxes everywhere, it was a mess and total darkness as I said. Out of the darkness appeared Philip on his bike, bless his heart, with a thermos of hot coffee and some apricot cake that he'd cooked himself. I thought just, 'This is the man for me.' We had wild passionate sex that night and quite a lot for some time after. Both my emotions and my sexuality were fully engaged, for the first time in my life.

At that stage he had just come back from Thailand from being a Buddhist monk. He was looking after the old monk at the Thebarton Temple, as well as doing his teaching diploma and acting as interpreter at the Queen Elizabeth Hospital. Philip is a very well organised person, he could juggle things like that.

Eventually I persuaded him to move in with me in 1984. That was just the most wonderful time, he helped me so much to get this place in order and not to waste money. I was still working full-time and so I was being ripped off a little bit by one particular tradesman, and Philip stopped that.

We went out together to the jeweller's and bought rings. I bought him a gold one and me a silver one, because I couldn't afford another gold one. He has given me the gold one since then. He was doing so much on the house. I'd take photos every step of the way and send them to my mother and she'd say, 'Aren't you doing anything? Philip seems to be doing everything'.

We went over to Sydney to visit her and I knew that she had at last accepted me as a gay man. She put us in a double bed and in the morning she brought in two cups of tea while we were still in bed together. For my mother that's the ultimate seal of approval and she liked Philip a lot. She knew that I'd struck the right one.

Then a year virtually to the day after Philip moved in, in 1985 they had a restructuring at the ABC and I lost my job. I had to do a Philip style of juggling things, and taking on several casual jobs. But it worked out really well for me because it gave me a chance to realise there was a wider world out there and more opportunities, which I used to try myself at different other things, which I hadn't had time to look at before, like writing infotainment. I had articles published in travel magazines and *DNA*. I had stories published in women's magazines. Thank goodness I'd stuck to my music studies when I was in Tasmania, as antidote to my desperate loneliness there. That stood me in good stead, because I was able to teach music privately as well. I also taught French and German conversation for a small language school. Eventually, later in 1985, I got a better paid job, teaching at the same technical college as Philip.

When we'd saved enough, we started to travel, at first to places that were then cheap, like Hungary, Spain, Indonesia and Italy. I like to know something of the language of most countries I travel in and so I learnt Italian, and a smattering of Spanish, Hungarian and Bahasa.

I had previously studied German privately with a teacher and had spent time in Germany twice, on scholarships, followed by several months studying music education in both Salzburg and Hungary and spending time with broadcasting organisations in those countries and also the BBC. As a result, working with my team, I was able to put new ideas into the music programs on my return. The children loved it, the ABC bureaucracy less so. That stood me in good stead because I was able to teach music privately as well.

That went on more or less like that, for twenty-three years, until we had our commitment ceremony in 2007 as part of the Feast Festival. My nephew said to me, 'So glad you're making a honest man out of Philip at last'. We always go to Pride and march in the Pride March, and last year we had our photo story on Facebook for Australians for Equality as part of the publicity for gay equal rights. So, there we are.

Philip

The political tangents, I guess, would be the ups and downs that we've had in Australia economically, the different recessions we've had, because there was that big recession after the share market crash in 1987. Then through '88, '89, '90, '91 and so on was really a tumultuous time in Australia in regards to interest rates going up through the roof. That's when Hugh and I had just got together and he'd lost his job, and that's when he came to work in the same workplace as me. That meant being totally out in the workplace, because we were a couple. People would ask, 'What did you do on the weekend?' It was extremely obvious that we were a couple and that was in a technical college. It didn't matter. I guess for a lot of people we were the first gay couple that they'd met and who did just normal things and had normal concerns, like interest rates, paying back the mortgage, going to get some stuff to do the floor or painting the walls, and things like that. Those were the extremely normal things we talked about and they could see then, so that's what a gay couple do. For a lot of people that whole idea was new, that two men could be living together and have bought a house and got the house in joint names, and that the bank accounts are in joint names, and the pronouns being used are 'we' and 'us' all the time. It was a bit of an eye-opener for a lot of people to see that, because the model for men back then very much was me-centred, and men were supposed to be in competition with other men. So it was quite an unusual thing to see that idea of a gay couple, who are working together towards a common goal, which at that stage was to make money. Kind of like two cavemen going out as a team, hunting a kangaroo, that sort of mentality, working together towards a goal.

I guess it was when I first saw this house that I knew, 'This is where I'm going to grow old and die.' I just knew that that's where I'm going to live, and Hugh also knew this is where he's going to live until he dies, too. We just knew that, it wasn't even anything we had to say to each other. There wasn't any decision to make. It was just there, we just knew this was the house we'll grow old in. It's a lot to do with home ownership, so we are extremely Australian that way, you know, that things very much rotate around home ownership.

I've been lucky that I've always known that I was gay and never seen anything particularly wrong with it, or anything particularly difficult about it. For me having gay sex is really easy and really enjoyable. I remember once I had sex with a guy and afterwards he felt so guilty, but that was just completely foreign to me, the idea of why he should feel guilty, because he was really into the sex while we were doing it, but afterwards felt terribly guilty about it. I just don't have that sort of backwards and forwards in my brain, for me it's alright to have sex and, it's all good fun and so have a nice giggle afterwards. 'Now let's have some lamb, let's have dinner'. It's all really easy for me, it's all straightforward.

The greatest support, as I say, that would be Hugh and my grandmother, because she could see that we'd settled down, my mother as well. My father had died by that stage. My mother saw that we'd settled down and they were very supportive of that, that we had a relationship, that we had a house, that everything was going well. There wasn't any undermining, there wasn't anybody who was jealous that we had that sort of relationship or that we had bought a house. The story I wanted to tell you about is about the success of that.

Hugh came to work at the same organisation as me, an organisation—a technical college—that you'd think might be perhaps a little bit homophobic or a little bit worried about some people who are not of the same sexuality as them. Actually no, that wasn't an issue at all. I think also they could understand that beggars couldn't be choosers. It was during a big recession and Hugh had lost his job at the ABC and that was a huge, huge concern to him, because he was very much of that generation who believed in the organisation. He came to the technical college and realised it was all about the money, because we had the house payments to make and people could see that yeah, we were just an ordinary couple with ordinary concerns. It was quite interesting to me to see that, because I was wondering how they would react when they saw that we were a couple. There were no arguments about that sort of thing, there were no arguments about he got such and such hours or I got such and such hours. It was all about how we need to get these hours to get this money.

Gabby

I always had the ideology to grow up, be married, have kids and live happily ever after. I did that in 1985, I got married and it lasted two and a half years, the marriage itself. I was working at a nightclub and this woman walked in, and from the first time I liked her. The second time she walked and I was just taken by her. I said if you know me well enough in two and a half years would you marry me? I'm one of these people like that. I had a beautiful wedding, my wedding was awesome. I had a normal wedding, what you would call a normal wedding. It cost about $15,000 this wedding, a lot of money. It was at the Greek church on Franklin Street. I got baptised Greek. There was no translation for Gary in the Greek translation to be baptised. So I was baptised Gabriel, hence Gabreiella.

It was after that my childhood ambitions and dreams disintegrated. I was at the point of virtually just wanting to kill myself, to knock myself off. It was deeply personal because I couldn't be that other and transition. Suddenly this dream of living happily ever after, kids in the family and the wife, that suddenly disappeared. Both things were a non-reality. My life was basically destroyed, so I was struggling right then and there to rebuild myself emotionally, because I cried for months. Probably two to three months after the marriage broke up and I was just distraught I couldn't see any future. I had two bags of clothes in the wardrobe and girl's clothes. She was aware of my cross dressing to a point. She knew I was bisexual.

Mahamati

I think I was happily married for some time, certainly the times at Nepabunna. We then lived briefly in Elizabeth, then in Glencoe in the South-East. David was the principal down at Glencoe Central School and I had really begun to resent being the mother at home with kids and not really having much of an identity. I hadn't worked. I was involved with all things school related and nothing that was me or my own. I think I probably found feminism and all that first, I guess. I was also becoming increasingly unhappy about being married and what that meant. I don't think I ever hated David but we certainly limped along, I guess. And, surprise, we had another child in Glencoe, Paul, much later than the others, and it was completely unexpected. I had birth control including an inner band loop. It was never planned at all. That of course sent me back into being full-time mother with a child.

We were living in Glencoe and David was extremely busy in the new open space ungraded study, the arts school that people came from all over the state and the world to see. We had lots of students visiting with us, we still have a lot of aboriginal connections. By this time the school was teaching aboriginal studies at university and teachers college. We would have aboriginal people coming to stay with us from the aboriginal community college doing their placements and also people from the Tiwi Islands coming for trips and tours. We lived next to the old school that was sort of kitted out as a basic living area for the masses. I had an interesting life but it wasn't my real life I don't think, I thought it was an extension of David's life.

I couldn't wait to escape some of that. Paul unfortunately suffered for that. He's the one that had measles, mumps, chickenpox, everything in the first year. The other two were at school and he wasn't, being younger. So I went to work. I got a job at St Mary's School in Mt Gambier in doing teacher's aide and library work. I had some very strong emotional friendships with the nuns and I guess what drew me was their connection to social justice work in the things that they were doing. The convent was changing radically. They were no longer cloistered or wearing veils all the time, and they wore ordinary clothes for schools. They also shared a lot of the compassion and interests in aboriginal studies so they had a good connection with David as well. We had many nights at our place with the aboriginal people, and some of the nuns playing music, drinking wine and parties and stuff, and I guess that was my first independent friendships apart from married couples. I guess that sustained me in staying married and there didn't seem to be a lot of choice then. So anyway, I stayed married and those friendships really helped that.

We eventually moved back to Adelaide. David was the principal at Rose Park Primary School. Following on from his work at Glencoe they had an open space unit, which Paul went right through as a student with David. It was an ungraded, open space school, considered quite radical at the time. He was given the opportunity to develop the open grade school. So kids could be doing grade two spelling and grade six maths and whatever the abilities went up and down the line. There was a lot more freedom.

He was at Rose Park when I got another job working at Saint Aloysius, another Catholic school associated with the Sisters of Mercy just like the sisters at Mount Gambier, so I had references from there. My job there was doing a lot of community work placements, work study, and helping out generally with those sorts of things at the school and I love that. Again I had really, really strong friendships with the nuns and major respect for the work that they were doing. One in particular, Anne Gregory, started the first women's shelter in Adelaide, at Elizabeth. I was fairly involved with that with her as was David. At that time we had a pet dog called Dunstan (after Don Dunstan), a Great Dane who was enormous. Dunstan would always go everywhere with us. At the shelter Anne had an invasion and it was really quite risky, she could have been killed and the women hurt. So we got her another Great Dane, which she called Julius or Sister Julius, to be her bodyguard. It was wonderful.

Those things, hearing the stories from the women from the shelter about the huge steps that they have made to get free of things and me being completely discontent with being married and wanting more, was where it started. I certainly wasn't interested sexually with David anymore and I started to be interested in women and I did have a few flings. It's hard to remember. There was just advertisements I'd seen in papers, things like that, we didn't have internet. I probably would have started a lot earlier if we had Internet. I sort of knew that the days of marriage were coming to an end somehow. But I also knew very well that it would never end from David's side. His parents had been divorced. His mother had married again and he didn't see his father much growing up, and it wasn't until his father died that he found out a lot more. We were still married at that time. David had always been told that his father didn't want anything to do with him, and he had been bought up by the stepfather whom he regarded as a father figure. We saw another side when we had to do things like go through his father's house with a stepbrother he had never seen and he had all these photos and things of David that he must have got from different relatives. The relatives said that he wanted David to have an ordinary life and not be torn between two people. David was never going to do that to his kids, so a break-up can never happen from David's point of view, even though he wasn't happy either, obviously.

So we stumbled along I think, then I found two things while he was at Rose Park. I began to find feminism through volunteering at the Adelaide Rape Crisis Centre. Then I thought I'd better get some qualifications so I went back to school and got mature age entry into university to do social work, and that gave me a lot more scope and a lot more direction. I became an administrator and counsellor of the Rape Crisis Centre during a time of the pretty heavy woman's movement in Adelaide and South Australia.

More shelters were opening up, and so did my friendship networks among women who were involved with shelters and sexual assault type work and feminism in general, and the women's health centres, where there was mental health groups for women. That's when I first got involved with women in terms of a sexual relationship. One of the women who I had met at one of the groups became the first person that I had a longer relationship with.

David didn't know or didn't want to know. I'm not sure even to this day if he knew. He would be away quite a bit and during school holidays I took the kids away on holidays in the caravan. We were virtually living very separate lives. I was working first at Saint Aloysius and the Rape Crisis Centre in various places. I began this relationship that sort of continued on and I eventually realised I've got to do something about that so we agreed to split. I didn't say the real reason why and again to this day I don't know if he really knew.

We agreed to split, the kids were terribly upset, they weren't happy. We never had anything like family courts or access agreements or anything like that. David to his grace said, 'I guess it's probably my turn', and it was true. He said, 'you've been the one who has been doing all the parenting and mothering while I've been doing career stuff so I guess it's my turn'. He virtually had the kids full time. They would come and go at mine as they wanted so that worked out as good as it could work in those circumstances. Certainly Paul (the youngest) was most affected and most unhappy. The other kids were twelve and thirteen or something like that. We split reasonably amicably in that we didn't have fights over things or money or kids or whatever. I was living at Norwood and was then free to get more involved with the Rape Crisis Centre and other women. The first woman I tried living together with for a year and a half, maybe two years and at some point in that progression I realised she wasn't the one and then I just continued having these short-term relationships for some time.

David D

My main goal as a young person was to do well academically. Later it was to achieve a partner. Academically I did well, becoming a solicitor. Partner-wise I had mixed success and could have tried harder. Up until middle age I was guilt ridden and confused about sexuality. This has led to five major breakdowns and four hospitalisations. HIV/AIDS became a major problem in 1985. My greatest support has come from my father, my sisters, friends Rosemary, Ian, Father Paul, Lawrence, Scottish Dave, Charlie, and my church and doctors.

It was a very small community in Darwin. In 1987 I became secretary of the Darwin Gay Society and we had parties and bar nights and things like that. We even went to male strippers with a lot of women but they didn't really like gay men being there. The scene in Darwin was quite small whereas in Melbourne in 1974 when I first left home I became involved with the fledging Melbourne Gay Society, which met in Latrobe Street upstairs above a cafe and I had much fun being seduced there. Police were busting parties, it was illegal in those days to be homosexual, not so much to be homosexual but to be engaging in homosexual activities. It was a bit of a haven this gay society and it was just before we had the mainstream gay saunas and gay clubs and things. They used to show wonderful videos and things, titillating, it was exciting and I dressed for the occasion a few times and had a good time with short shorts and open T-shirts and stuff like that.

They abolished the sodomy laws and homosexuality became more accepted over the years. We had in Sydney the amazing Signal Bar. It had themes such as the Village People and characters within that. It was exciting to have these clubs but then there was a further evolution in the last ten years where gay people are just ordinary people now accepted in straight venues. Except in Adelaide we find we have no real gay pub. I must say I think young people don't want to have labels, they just want to be themselves. So things have changed a lot, fortunately for older gay guys in Adelaide there's some really good things such as Queen of Tarts in Hutt Street, absolutely fabulous, every second Wednesday, Catalyst for over fifties, dinners at the Arab Steed Hotel and of course the Adelaide Gay and Lesbian Choir has been marvellous for me. I'm still very much involved in gay life but I find young people can be very snotty with their ageism and not friendly. I believe this is really prevalent in Sydney where there is a lot of antagonism between young gay men and older gay men, which is a shame. I have a partner, well sort of partner, in Sydney, Lawrence. We communicate every day, email in the morning and phone call in the evening, and we've been doing that for seven or eight years and he tells me about this ageism in Sydney. It's a generalisation, not all young people are like that but it can be a social rejection by young people of older gay men, which is a shame really.

Not so much lesbians. I can't remember any lesbians in the Melbourne Gay Society in 1974, it was all gay men. There was nothing illegal about lesbian relationships, they didn't have the stigma that we had. I think that the Society was good to them, especially for young people to get a bit of confidence and acceptance of their own personality and sexuality.

In 1989 I was a bit manic and I was feeling like a bit of fun one night so after Dad went to bed at South Melbourne I got some clobber on, some lycra shorts and women's teddy I had on, and a jacket. I was close to Albert Park Lake and I walked down to Albert Park Lake and I was sort of looking for fun but I got down to one end of the lake and this police van was pulling up. I ran away because of my experience during my first breakdown in 1974 when I was taken to the Rundle by police paddy van and I was a bit fearful of police. When they approached me at Albert Park they put their lights on high beam and I started to run. They ran after me got me to the ground and kicked me, my nose was bleeding they got me in the paddy wagon and drove over all the curbs and I was screaming.

I was still distressed when they got me to the South Melbourne police station. My nose was bleeding for three hours. I refused to go and a big six-foot-seven man came from police headquarters on St Kilda Road, I think he was the police medical officer. He was eyeballing me and wanting me to go home. Eventually I agreed to go home after two or three hours. When I first got to the police station they got me in the cells they got me to pull my pants down and bend over and hosed me with a hose. So I eventually agreed to go home. I told them my dad was at home. They went over all the curbs again. I was screaming and they woke Dad up.

The next day I was admitted to the psychiatric ward of the Prince Henry Hospital on St Kilda Road. I was there for two or three weeks and when I got home a sergeant came around with a summons that I had assaulted and kicked the police. At that time I was involved with the AIDS Council and they've financed one of the best criminal barristers to represent me. He wrote to the police and immediately a sergeant came around and said 'if you sign a document that you won't take action against us we won't take action against you'. I'd been so ill that I didn't have the strength to say no so I signed it. The sergeant told me that the two officers who assaulted me were nineteen and twenty-one years of age, and one had since left the police force and I said I'm not surprised. My gay doctor, whose practice was at Middle Park, the main gay medical practice for Melbourne at the time, said 'David there's been so many police bashings you are lucky you didn't lose your life'. It was a bit like a Dr Duncan episode. Very awesome, thank God for the AIDS Council.

My dad was very protective of me with my sexuality. I think that despite being a communist and a narrow-minded Methodist, he was still protective of me and he would defend me; like when I was going to be married to my secretary and my wife-to-be's mother got on the phone after going through my drawers and said to Dad 'does your son have a sexual problem'. When Dad replied 'the only problem is you', she hung up and I think that was protective. I had probably told dad that with my future wife Jan I was open and said that I was bisexual and that I couldn't change myself but I would work at a happy marriage.

Later in life from 1989 to 1999 I lived with him because of my breakdowns and my other illnesses. We both became devoted to going to the Uniting Church and when I first got to Darwin we were wanting to worship at Nightcliff Uniting Church. I was a little bit manic with my highs and went around the church saying I am bipolar and I've got HIV. They had a meeting to decide whether we could worship there. Dad was always protective of me with people and it worked out okay in the end.

I nearly died through ill health in the nineties and the church became a great solace for me. I haven't been one to force my spiritual beliefs on other people but just the feeling of solace and comfort that I got from Christianity helped me a hell of a lot to be more settled, especially with my mental health. The Uniting Church is an amazing church. Its motto is 'Unity in Diversity'. There were three main Uniting Churches in Darwin. Nightcliff Uniting was the social justice and the lefties, Casuarina Uniting Church in which you had the happy clappy evangelical service that was very condemning of homosexuality, and the Darwin Uniting in the conservative tradition. Years later I am now worshipping in Adelaide at Pilgrim Uniting Church and they have three different services. The eight o'clock in the morning, which is a fairly down to earth communion service every Sunday with breakfast afterwards. The nine-thirty, which I go to, has the social justice people and it is very modern and very spontaneous. Then you have the eleven o'clock, which is conservative and traditional. The minister has to preach and relate to three completely different theologies.

When I first went to Darwin I talked to the Nightcliff Uniting Church parishioners about my mental health and other bad health issues. They thought I was in a relationship with Dad and held a meeting to decide whether we could worship there. In South Melbourne when I first started going to the Uniting Church there was a young woman and her husband who gave me some pretty bad stares, that was the worst of it really. We had a minister there, when I was bashed by the police, who went to the police and apologised for my homosexuality. Instead of trying to make it better he made it worse and he was a very conservative man. There were two ministers there. The other minister was Joe Fraser, he was a social justice man, absolutely lovely. He visited me in hospital in South Melbourne after being bashed and the breakdown with huge bouquets of freesias from his garden, absolutely magnificent.

Mahamati

At this point after I left I'd taken Paul to India for a year and we sort of traipsed around places that he wouldn't have been before. When I got back I got involved with sending kids to the alternative unit at Rose Park for quite some time. They'd had meditation groups open to the public that really drew me, as well as feminism. But I was a bit uncomfortable to be following the male guru when I'm espousing this different view about women and wanting rights. So I went to the meditations but never got totally involved. Several of my other lesbian friends did and I guess by that time I had quite a wide range of lesbian friends and networks and there was a lot on in Adelaide at the time. A lot of unorganised social things that happened but don't happen now, it was good. It was probably some of the best times I think. There'd be discussion groups, consciousness-raising groups, lesbian studies groups, pub nights, women's dances, women's nude swimming, women's performing nights, concerts. Some of the groups might number several hundred, and several hundred people would rock up for the International Women's Day dance, probably more like a thousand. There might be two hundred people in the lesbian bushwalking group which would overlap with members of the lesbian tennis group. The networks crisscrossed as did friendships and lovers and ex-lovers. We used to joke that if you went to Central

Market on Saturday morning then you'll find out who went home with who on Friday night because they'd all rock up at the chairs on Saturday morning with who they went home with last night.

I certainly knew some gay men but not well. I was doing some work at the rape crisis centre with a particular therapy called Radix therapy, which is working with the body as well as talking about emotions. It was considered useful at the time with people expressing what they had been through. One of my lesbian friends who was also involved with ashram had been doing the Radix training in Pune, where you can go to study and learn the course for three months. We both decided we were going to go and do this, but she was unable to go on because she worked independently as a masseur and a therapist and the bank wouldn't give her a loan because she was a single woman and that was still a problem. She didn't have a regular income even though she was doing quite well. She still encouraged me to do it, and I thought 'I don't know. I don't really want to get involved with ashram stuff really' and she said 'you probably don't have to, just go along and do the course'.

I had been to India before so I wouldn't have a problem adjusting to being in India. I went and I found out that you actually cannot do the course unless you do the morning 6am meditation and the evening one at eight o'clock. They won't take you otherwise as the course can be quite challenging and emotional so they use those meditations for dealing with that and so I signed up for it. I got totally immersed in it and didn't believe I could possibly get involved following a male guru but I did.

So I stayed there and I finished the course, including the process where we take another name, which is how I became known as Mahamati. I worried for the next few months about how I would tell everyone at work and the Rape Crisis Centre I was coming back with a new name. Most people knew about the movement and it was quite infamous at the time. They were called the Orange People and at one stage I wore all orange and had to proclaim my following for Rajneesh. It was quite infamous and very unpopular in India because he espoused a lot of free sex, then no limits, and free expression as much as it possibly can in any way possible. The Indian government wasn't particularly pleased with him so they'd often refuse to give visas to Westerners with Indian names. We were advised not to change our names legally because we might have a hassle getting visas so I did never change it legally but people have known me as Mahamati ever since I came back from India.

I wondered how I was going to deal with that so what I ended up doing was having a huge party at the Rape Crisis Centre and having a renaming party with about forty to fifty close friends. The Ma which denotes woman and then there's a prefix which is Santhosh and then Mahamati, you're only called by the last part and the prefix is just the prefix. Santhosh means contentment and Mahamati is supposed to mean great mind, so one of the things to aspire to. In the old days he would choose your name if you had been there for long enough and thought that you were ready for it. People are still going, which is quite amazing as he has been dead for some time. At one point I was going to go back and live there forever, well not forever, but as long as I could afford and then come back and work and then go back again. It worked out incredibly well in that when I was working at Rape Crisis there was another woman Dr Casey who is still a very good friend. Not a lesbian but very feminist and we worked at Rape Crisis together for a very long while. She was also very drawn to India for different reasons and different people but I'd often be working at Rape Crisis for six months in an administration job and coordinator job and then go off to India and then she would come back and take the job. This sort of played out over a couple of years with us alternating and on one of those trips coming back from India I thought okay well what now. I think the Rape Crisis Centre had to close and got absorbed into the sexual assault centre and government services. I came back and thought I'd better look for a job, and the job I was drawn to was at the AIDS Council.

It was in 1990 and it was doing a project for the women partners of bisexual and gay men at that time of the epidemic with the fear that all the heterosexuals were going to get AIDS. So there was this two-year needs analysis with a person in Queensland doing one part and I was doing another part of it for a year. We put stuff together and I got the job for a second year doing a national training project for healthcare people and practitioners about the needs of women who find themselves in this situation and how to work with men who are in that situation. That was my first real working and good experience with gay men and I loved it. I didn't find it confronting, I did in terms of the deaths but not in terms of the issues. When I was still working at Saint Aloysius there was a gay teacher there and we found each other at some level and were talking about the issues happening and the status of gay man. I tried to find out what I could just by reading; it was only the newspapers in those days. Around the same time gay men in South Australia had organised the Gay Men's Health response to HIV prior to it becoming the AIDS Council, an incorporated body, and they worked out of a place in Carrington Street that was also a chat line.

I had also been doing things like lesbian line and there were all these questions coming in about whether lesbians can get AIDS and so little known at the time. So once I got into the AIDS Council system it was great because I could go do lots of training and there were training courses in so many different aspects of HIV and AIDS. I became quite knowledgeable on the issues and I liked the connections and the friendships with gay men. At the time I came across Ian Purcell, who recently died, who was in the library at that time and very much fostering the biggest gay and lesbian and HIV library in Australia there. It was at Darlington House where people would come all the time to use it and it was fantastic in terms of atmosphere and sense of community. Another very good friend who's in Victorian human rights now was there at the same time and we did some training together for our own gay and lesbian counselling line. It was my first involvement into the broader gay community separate from the lesbian community.

Before HIV and AIDS there was very little mix between lesbians and gay men. There were some gay nights at some of the pubs and I had been sometimes, but I didn't feel a great connection nor did most of the lesbians. I think most of the lesbians were very separatist. There has been some lesbian pubs, lesbian bars at different times popping up and dying off and coming back again but there wasn't a wider LGBT community. A lot of my lesbian friends questioned that I was doing all this stuff for gay men and what about all the lesbians. It was too confrontational to say so directly but there were certainly questions about why I would want to get involved with gay men? I was still working part time when I got the job at Second Story (the youth health centre) running the young lesbian coming out groups. There used to be a drop-in at nights and they also ran structured programs like In and Out just like places in Sydney and other groups do. I ran the young lesbians group, it was called LBW (lesbian bisexual women) and some of the young women who were in that group I still have a connection with and they're some of the leaders in the equality movements and trans movements and things now. It's quite rewarding to see them doing all this wonderful stuff.

While I was there doing that we also got a contract to write a manual for teachers called Block Out: Challenging Homophobia. It was for teachers to better understand teaching issues for young teens and, Kenton Penley Miller in particular, has done a lot of work and research on the incidence of youth suicide particularly among young gay men and was very passionate about that. We tried to address some of those issues for teachers and social workers to understand better. First we did this Block Out program, and at the time the Education Minister was quite enlightened and gave us money and we did workshops all around the state, which was great. We met a lot of teachers and youth workers, and clergy, and all sorts and did these workshops that was quite successful and I was continuing to do a day a week at the AIDS Council for the women partners of gay men and also had a couple of women's groups going. Stephen House, who's now a playwright, also worked there for a while and we did a group there called Pillow Talk for bi men and their wives. We did that for a while.

After that I had some job issues. I think a friend was working at what was then Adelaide Central Mission (now Uniting Communities) and she was successful in getting a one-year innovative grant happening to operate what has become Bfriend. I applied for the job and got the job coordinating Bfriend with a young man named Henry. He only stayed for a little while before he went back to Melbourne. I continued with Bfriend for three or four years as the female liaison and had different co-workers coming in at different times as the male worker. At that time it only catered to gay men and lesbians because the trans visibility was really zilch in South Australia and we had felt that trans visibility was so little that we didn't have the volunteers to be the Bfrienders for the people coming in.

At its height, Bfriend was really fantastic. We had two hundred volunteers aged from seventeen to seventy and we had everyone from fourteen-year-old kids to married people coming in there. We ran group after group training people. Some of them were women in the lesbian groups, or gay men could come across and they'd do the Bfriend training too, until we had two hundred people that we could link up to somebody. We'd run groups as well like married and wondering. How the Church let me do that I have no idea. At the time the woman who was in charge of that area of human resources was a wonderful person who had a really strong passion for that work and for the parents of lesbians, so we had a parents group as part of Bfriend as well for parents to befriend other parents and help them be more supportive to their kids. That worked really well.

The parents group was much smaller than PFLAG. PFLAG wasn't happening here, it wasn't in existence then. This was quite a small group, we'd only have a couple dozen parents. Some of them were fantastic. There was one particular couple who were the pillars of their church in Jamestown or some country town. They had two gay sons and one lesbian daughter. They were just fantastic when we had some parents worrying what was going to happen to their child, we'd link them up and it was just a great role model for parents who are really floundering and questioning and wondering what they could really do.

As I said I had this ongoing involvement with the AIDS Council for quite some time. Then another funding crisis happened. I have never been bored but I've had lots of funding crises and Bfriend looked like it was going under. We had this innovation grant that had been extended with three more years left and after that it was really uncertain. It did look like it would not get any more money from the mission or health department. So I applied for jobs and I got two. I got one at Southern Women's Health which had a lesbian health project, and I got a good job at Queensland AIDS Council in Cairns. I was in another relationship then, which had been going on for some years. It wasn't going well and we'd bought a house in Semaphore, where a lot of lesbians lived at the time. It was cheaper housing so a lot of women moved to those areas and were just starting to get paid work. A lot of the lesbians who had worked as volunteers for years and years and years were now getting paid jobs and could afford mortgages and could get housing and Semaphore was one of the places. There were lesbian owned restaurants and coffee shops and bookshops and stuff like that.

A lot of women didn't have the qualifications in this period. They might have gone back to study. I certainly know some who did get qualifications so they could get work. A lot were volunteers because they didn't get paid work and others would volunteer because of personal ethics and passion for things and it was much easier to get the dole then. There were a lot of share houses in Adelaide, there'd be four or five women in a share house so they could afford to live reasonably comfortably on the dole. You weren't hassled like you are now to the same extent. There was lots of community work when you were on the dole and people then sort of drifted into paid work.

1990s

The Commonwealth Migration Act 1958 Amended
In 1991 a new category of visa was introduced into Australia. It wasn't exclusively designed for same-sex couples but as a result, an Australian was able to sponsor their same-sex partner to migrate to Australia. The 'Interdependency' category of visa overcame the hurdle that existed in which spouses, or prospective spouses, were able to sponsor their foreign partner when it came to migrating to Australia.[16] This change in the law made it possible for same-sex partners to become sponsors but it didn't clear a lot of the potential issues down the line such as having 'same-sex' listed on your visa when applying for work. Through consecutive governments the ability to sponsor a partner has been made more difficult, and reverted back to previous positions.

The Australian Government Begins Slow March Out of People's Private Lives
In the 1990s Australia had signed up to certain clauses of human rights as decided by international bodies, in particular the United Nations. As a result, in 1994 the federal government introduced the Human Rights

(Sexual Conduct) Act 1994 with the purpose 'to implement Australia's international obligations under Article 17 of the International Covenant on Civil and Political Rights'.[17] The legislation made it legal for consenting adults in private to be involved in any sexual conduct they wanted. This cemented Australian law making sex acts between any consenting adults legal in all states and territories and sought to overrule some existing state laws. It finally allowed adults to do what they pleased in private.

However, Tasmania continued to hold onto its laws that made homosexuality illegal and cementing itself as the last state to remove such laws. Gay rights groups in Tasmania used the federal government act and took Tasmania to the High Court to force the state government to change its laws. There was an attempt by Tasmanian Greens to pass the law in 1996 that failed. Another attempt in 1997 passed the state's upper house by one vote.[18]

Gabby

I had done so much. I've worked in the hospitality industry thirty-five years. I started off in little stands to nightclubs to corporate VIPs in aviation in America. I don't have a great big goal set for myself but if I find something I'm curious about or if someone says it's something I can't do then you can find that I'm more likely to do it. Me going over to America was because people always said I wouldn't.

I'd won a court case, a discrimination case against someone. It started when I made page two of *The Advertiser* and the headline was 'local boy meets Madonna'. I worked at that time because I'm always in multiple jobs. I was working in the meat industry, separating hearts, lungs, kidneys, pancreas, gall bladder from cattle. I spent all day covered in blood. I did multiple jobs, so I'd finish there and go help a mate in a cafeteria and that's how I met Madonna. When people read the story the next day I started to get discrimination in the workplace. I was getting called gay, queer, poofter. I was being ostracised. My car was broken into. My car windows were wound down at night on rainy nights so that my car would get full of water. My locker got broken into, my knives and everything would be stolen. Hot water hoses would be sabotaged with clamps so that as soon as you turn it on it would burst. So I took them to court and eventually they settled so that gave me the money to go overseas. Settlement is winning. If there is no case you don't settle.

If you settled it means you've done something wrong in my eyes.

So people said to me 'oh, you're never gonna go overseas'. He (my partner at the time) was close to passing away and I went over to be with him and I came back eighteen months later. I was going every three months, and I ended up coming back eighteen months later. In that eighteen months the triple cocktail therapy came out. I have a different way in life to him. I don't like junk food—I don't mind it but I don't like it. I'd rather eat proper food and I got him very healthy. I got him back into full productivity and back into working—not in that eighteen months but eventually he was working again. I got into aviation because he worked in the VIP corporate aviation industry, so I had a back door in. I worked in services, doing the catering to supply food for them on corporate flights. For example, if they wanted prawn cocktail VIP catering would charge say about sixty to seventy dollars for that and you've got to supply it. Well, if you're clever, you'll use every resource you can to reduce your costs. So, I'd go straight to Cosco. I had a Costco card and I'd buy a prawn platter but that's not how I'd present the plate. I would take it home and take all the prawns, remove the sauce and put it on a silver platter with nice fresh lettuce, redress it put some alfoil on it and sell it at sixty bucks when it cost me ten. I'd also deal with all the cleaning in between. Every tea towel, every napkin, that's a dollar fifty each. For sixty napkins and that money adds up. I've only flown three times. I flew two Cessnas up into LA airspace to see what it was like actually flying a plane, instead of using a flight simulator. The third time the auto pilot was on technically but I was flying because I was in the pilot seat and that was twenty-five thousand feet above the Pacific.

They were very interesting because the people who I associated with over in LA were more in television or in the entertainment type industry, so they were all saying to me 'you're a handsome hunk' and I said nah. That's how my logic was. At first I didn't want to be in movies. I just wanted to enjoy a bit of LA. Eventually they twisted my arm. So basically I went to over two hundred agencies in Los Angeles. When I say agencies I mean people who claim they can get you into movies. I was listening to all those stories and the consistent theme to most of them, about ninety percent of the agencies, was they wanted money out of you to get head shots and they'd guarantee you everything. They'd get you in to Bazaar, they'd get you into Vogue, get you into movies, but they wanted money out of you. Just three companies didn't want a lot of money from me, all they wanted was a headshot—a Polaroid—and a small fee. My total investment was ninety-five dollars for the three companies.

Eventually I started working in a few sets. I started to get to know people. My name started to get around and started to get into different sets. So instead of just being cast in a normal B-grade movie suddenly I found myself on City of Angels with Meg Ryan and Nicolas

Cage. I'm an Angel and I walk down a corridor to kids in bed. I started working on other movies, Dance With Me and a few others. And then I started getting into TV as well because I started to know people and was getting called back. So, I ended up on ER, Chicago Hope, and that lead to 90210 and Melrose Place.

I still dealing with him (ex-partner) and he had multiple issues. He was possessive, jealous, and alcoholic. He was extremely jealous. He had this beautiful young man (me) and he was afraid that young man was going to walk. It was very hard to deal with. He was constantly drinking to the point that I couldn't store alcohol at home. I couldn't even have a bottle of vodka in the cupboard because when I'd go to drink it, the bottle would be full of water. So, I was dealing with a gay man who was a slob and an excessive alcoholic. Every day he had to drink. He'd be equally nasty with words. I couldn't deal with it a couple of times. I'd pack up and head to the neighbour's house to cry my guts out. It was very hard. He was on his last wishes of death. What do you do and how do you handle someone like that? He's abusive but you love him. He's as an alcoholic and has got HIV. You can't deal.

He attacked me one night, he smashed me in the head and my instant reaction was to just launch one back. It cost me eleven-and-a-half thousand dollars just hitting him once. I was not a small boy. I was that big guy you saw in the photographs. I had huge strength and I shattered his jaw. How do you deal? Mentally it's just fucked in the head. After that there was nowhere I could go. I was a stranger basically. Other than the immediate few friends I had over there, there wasn't much I could do. I could fly home but it can take forty-eight hours to get home and that's an expensive flight. He had his support network because he had gay groups in Los Angeles and that. I don't go relying on people I never have wanted to say help, help, help. I'm usually the one helping everyone else.

The relationship ended because of his alcoholism. I had just had enough. I was battling my own issues. I was one hundred and forty kilograms there was no way I could fit into my girl clothes, which I had in a bag, anymore so I was getting more and more mentally exhausted and frustrated for myself. It was just building up and I was not getting any relief. My outlets were just shrinking away. There wasn't any stimulation or break from being that person. I had to go. I found myself being selfish—that's how I felt, that's how I regarded it—as being selfish, even though it wasn't but I regarded it so. I had to leave him and he died eighteen months later. He died in a hospital bed by himself. The house we had together was a beautiful home but by then it was just trash. There was cat litter everywhere. He hadn't done anything. He just drank piss and died. That was sad. And then his family destroyed the will and I got nothing even though we were partners. What do you do? You just move on. I rebuilt several times over the years.

Travis

Probably one of the critical things was actually being in a relationship and having a partner. Saying publicly that I prefer to have sex with men rather than women, particularly in the eighties and nineties, was way too difficult to do and I think was inviting judgement. Whereas saying this is my partner is an easier, normal, rational, more coherent way of publicly identifying myself. Nevertheless, I don't think I went looking for a partner. It just happened, in San Francisco. I certainly had to be public about it then, so yes, I did have to tell my family and did have to get my partner into Australia. I had to convince immigration that I was in the relationship. So it was not necessarily loudly but certainly definitively coming out of the closet. Being in a relationship was significant. We met in 1992. It was pre-Howard. The ability for same-sex partnerships to get visas was relatively recent and there were helpful supportive groups like the Gay and Lesbian Immigration Task Force that had a lot of expertise and provided a lot of support in processing the endless documentation.

Professionally, I graduated in medicine, didn't become an ENT specialist as I had planned, which possibly was a good thing in terms of doing something professionally really good and really satisfying and really productive. Fifteen years at a government youth program working with adolescents and particularly supporting boys in their journey was a really fun, really big achievement. When I was working in the hospital there was a sixteen-year-old boy with leukaemia, and he taught me I wasn't scared of adolescents. He died but I regarded him as one of my most important teachers. I also worked supporting and facilitating people to achieve what they wanted to achieve and do the best they can. Training junior doctors in adolescent health is something I'm particularly proud of because there are a few who I have worked with who have gone on to way surpass me in qualifications around adolescent work, so being in a position to advise and support them and confirm that they're doing something really good. I'm proud.

As one of my juniors put it, I've got a problem with authority. I've got this obstinate, anti-status quo, anti-authority streak and I pretty constantly found myself in conflict with management and superiors, because in my opinion I was right and they were wrong. So one of the blocks I came up against was working through the politics of all that, working through the politics of general practice, so I wound up not being nearly as qualified as I should be and that then limits my career options. So yeah, dealing with managers and bureaucracy, that's the stuff I've always found particularly difficult.

I'd always wondered about homophobia from individuals that blocked my career progress. I'm not really aware of being stopped or blocked in anything because of my sexuality or relationships. I might have just missed it but it's not something I've seen.

There is another achievement that's worth mentioning, again it's with police. This was in the late nineties. My relationship was falling apart and I was walking along the beach when I saw a young guy in the sand dunes and went over to talk to him. After some conversation and asking questions I placed my hand on his knee and he pulled out his badge and arrested me for indecent assault. The whole police operation was obviously intended to humiliate their targets, so they'd be handcuffed, taken to the police station, photographed, fingerprinted, and put into a cell. I think they expected me to plead guilty to the charge and get it over with as quickly as possible and get out of there, but that was really not an option for me. So I got some very good legal assistance.

At around the same time there was a discussion between police and gay community leaders about police harassment and entrapment at beats and violence against gays that was not being addressed. The police had demanded evidence of this police behaviour for them to start taking it seriously. They wanted names, dates and places, so with my permission they used the example of my situation. That was one of a number of instances at the time in the mid-to-late nineties when in South Australia the attitude of police changed, the rules around policing beats changed, the focus of the police shifted to dealing with violence rather than just harassing people for being gay. That was, I suppose more my problem with authority. I wasn't just going to accept what they were handing out.

In the end there were no charges. In the same beat operation there was a straight boy from Sydney on the beach with his girlfriend. They'd come to Adelaide on a mystery flight and he pulled down his pants to brush the sand off his bum and found himself under arrest. The lawyer got him off all charges and back home and then he said to the police, 'well you let of the straight man so you're not going to discriminate are you?'. I keep thinking back on it and think it was absolute nonsense, if there was anything indecent to be done I had a house a short walk away.

David D

Later in life from 1998 to 2003 my second gay relationship was with David Geraud. David was amazing and he was very involved with the Adelaide Gay and Lesbian Counselling Service. He would work on Christmas Day and take his lunch in there. He was a lovely man and he wrote over three hundred love letters to me and he would write to anyone in a distinctive old-fashioned style, including to politicians. He was very strong with aboriginal rights as well as gay rights and he was very well known. An example of his quaint old-fashioned style was, 'Dear David, I hope this missive finds you well', and in the end he would say 'I am your dear friend, yours faithfully'. He was very slight, he'd been mangled in a motorbike accident early in his life and he had chronic rheumatoid arthritis. In the end he was taking high dosages of the new drug for osteoarthritis, Celebrex. He died of an aneurysm, they found very soon afterwards that high doses could cause aneurysms.

He was an amazing man. He was a member of the Labor Party too, as I was. His friend Gilly was Bob Hawke's secretary and I used to meet Gilly and Bob at the Adelaide Bob Hawke Memorial Lectures at the town hall. When David died he told me Gilly has given me this book called *Australian Prime Ministers* by Michelle Grattan that had five prime ministers' signatures in it. Gilly said I should go to David's house and get it for myself.

I think there was more gossip with John Gorton because when I was breaking up with Paulie, John would arrive at the house in a female chauffeured Commonwealth car and I met John, Sir John. He said to me Paulie's house was not very well designed. He was very snobbish because it was a very nice house. Paulie gave me his Italian mountain ash futon bed. I often thought 'Sir John's been in that bed'. I ended up giving it to the Salvos in Darwin, and the Salvos bloke said to me 'I can just imagine me and the missus in this bed'.

Gabby

It was my time to come out, there was no way I was going to let that shit happen. I'm not that little boy or young man anymore. I've gone through eras when I've been a hundred-and-forty kilogram man, and I could pick up a hundred-and-twenty kilogram deadlift. Throughout transition my goal was to not lose any of those abilities. I wasn't coming out to be glam and pretty. I came out and did my transition to be totally complete within myself. Not for anyone else's ideology or anyone else's perceived image, that was not what it was about for me. It was my own personal development, my own personal growth. There was no way I was going to allow anyone to hinder, prohibit, or get in my way. Nor was I not going to allow anyone to hinder anyone else I knew from that day onwards. I was not going to accept anyone getting hindered or harassed for being transgender. There was just to no way.

I had a goal I set myself. I had to lose the weight. There was no way I could transition that way and be healthy. It was just asking too much. My body was in its forties then, and it's just not workable to hammer it how I was going to hammer it with hormones, so to do what I needed to do and be healthy at the same time then there had to be some sacrifices. So the first goal I set myself was to get below eighty kilos. I got to seventy-eight. But my time limit was running out because I wanted to have my vagina by the time I was fifty. I did not want to see my fiftieth birthday without my vagina. Simple as that. It was a new era, a new life. I'd done fifty years the other way, and now this was my time, so that's what I did. I set myself two years. That two years became a wholly different era in my life, because then I was dealing with other people's ideologies, other people's perceptions. Before then what I was dealing with was the heterosexual community and all their discriminations or their phobias and whatever I was dealing with mentally, sorting out where I fit and how I fit. Then suddenly I was dealing with a psychiatrist and bureaucrats who were going to try and hinder me at every single turn to stop me doing it. In the process I came across a gay man I knew for a long time as a kid. He didn't even recognise me or remember me as a boy, but I remembered him, and I had to tell him about myself to get your paperwork I needed to move forward. The gay community had a monopoly is the only way to look at it, they controlled it as a monopoly. They control the events, the little events, they're very close, all of them.

I knew I was going to have forms. I had a good doctor, I've had my own doctor all my life, so he knew I was of sound mind and sound body so he gave me my hormones. So I started with hormones, but to go and have sex change surgery you've got to have paperwork. You've got to meet certain criteria. The doctors who have to sign off on that paperwork are commonly referred to as gatekeepers in the trans community. The terminology is gatekeeper because if he doesn't give you the golden key you can't go get your sex change. If one doctor didn't refer you forward to the next doctor then the process stopped. And the doctors involved all had each other's backs for years and years. My experience with the doctor was very interesting. I was right at the beginning of transitioning, and so I wasn't glamming up. Most people perceive that if you're transgender you're going to glamour up, you're gonna be throwing the make-up on, the frilly dresses, the high heels. You'll be going, 'oh dear, hello dear', and camping up the way you talk. That's an ideology and perception that the doctor still had, that if you're going to be allowed to transition then you have to do all this.

I'm a woman. I'm a bitch. Simple. I'm not a lady. I'm not a princess. I'm just a woman, an Australian woman. The only real political issue that I found affected me to do with transition was the proposed legislation that Julia Gillard and Kevin Rudd put forward that made it easier for trans people to get passports and change ID without going through so much bureaucratic crap like you had to before. That made it a lot easier to go somewhere like Thailand as you're already a woman on your passport, not a man. Because when you go to Thailand you could have that image completely renewed, you're a woman in every way when you have the operation, but they're going to address you by the name on your passport. Thailand was always my ultimate goal. I always saw Thailand as the place that was going to help me take the next step. I always knew that Thailand was the place I needed to be.

I had thought of Germany because of Christine Jorgensen and Denmark because of the operations that happened there. Thailand wasn't really well known back then. But now Thailand's cosmetic industry has grown. Thailand was also cheaper.

The 2000s

Over the course of the 2000s Australian states and territories introduced varying legislation to recognise and protect the rights of LGBTIQ people and their families. It included changes such as adoption rights, recognition of overseas same-sex marriages and having partners listed as such on death certificates. Before a public vote on same-sex marriage was even thought of, the majority of state and territory leaders were in favour of equal rights for LGBTIQ couples and families, however conservative and Christian elements within the federal government sought to hold off such changes under the guise of 'religious freedoms'.

Howard Amends the Marriage Act
Several same-sex couples attempted to take advantage of the vagueness in the Australian Federal Marriage Act 1961 by applying for marriage licenses. The Howard Government in 2004 under its conservative Christian brand sought to prevent marriages between same-sex couples and successfully introduced legislation that changed the act to explicitly state that marriage is between a man and a woman. In the background of the

amendments the government claimed:

'The Government's haste to have the current Bill passed appears to be linked to two applications filed in court to have same sex marriages performed within the laws of another country recognised under Australian law. This Bill amends the *Marriage Act 1961* to prevent the recognition of same-sex marriages in Australia, even where the marriage has been performed under the laws of another country which does recognise this type of union.

'In addition the Government has also indicated that the need for Parliament to give its immediate attention to the current Bill is related to expressions of significant community concern about the possible erosion of the institution of marriage. It is the Attorney-General's opinion that Parliament's quick action is needed to address these community concerns.'[19]

It was from that moment that the marriage equality movement became solidly established and the push for this amendment to be overturned began. The amendment stating marriage is between a man and a woman was moved by the Attorney-General Philip Ruddock, and passed easily through both the house and the senate.

Rudd Government Passes Sweeping Pro-LGBTIQ Legislation

In 2008 the Rudd Government passed a package of law reforms that opened up new opportunities for LGBTIQ Australians. The majority of these related to family and taxation and eased the path to accessing entitlements for people in same-sex couples. The laws included changes to immigration laws, citizenship, child support, family law, taxation, and social security. It made it easier for partners of recently deceased people to access their superannuation, veteran's entitlements and family assistance.[20]

Thomas

When looking back, because I was adopted I always wanted children of my own. It was a big thing that I never knew my parents, that was huge. So I was going overseas with three mates and my girlfriend at the time was going with some of her friends as well. They all pulled out so we decided to travel together. This was a no-no back in the seventies. We were told that you don't do something like that unless you get married, so we did. I didn't regret getting married as I said as I think if I hadn't I wouldn't be alive today. I'm a bit of a rebel and I probably would have moved to Sydney and ended up swinging around and a lot of people around my age who went down that way got nasty diseases. I just sort of know I'm a bit of a naughty boy.

Vietnam played a big part of my life. Luckily my number wasn't called so I decided to travel overseas. I didn't really take any part in the protest or the political movements as I worked in the Bank as I said, that was a no-no. There was a certain time I thought I was living a lie and decided to come out and my wife wasn't happy but she supported me, and my two beautiful children said they knew that I was gay. Work colleagues have been pretty good with that as well. A lot of work colleagues actually come and watch me do drag shows now. It's just so good that you can be at work and don't have to lie or tell falsehoods. This is what I am, this is how I'm going to live, and it's just lifts a burden off you when you actually come out and be who you are.

At a certain time of my life I decided I was living a lie and had to come out. My wife wasn't very happy of course, but she thought she can't compete with a penis. I think if I left her for another woman, that would have been worse. I know it's hard to lose a spouse whichever way you go, but I think it was easier for her understanding that she just could not be what I needed in a partner. When I told my kids they said, 'Dad, we knew you were gay'. Kids aren't stupid. My wife asked if I was having an affair with a friend and I was sick of the lies, so I told her I was and came out. Which meant I then had to tell the kids, and I thought they'd hate me but they were fine. They were just fantastic. I figure they were bought up to respect everybody for what they are and who they are and not judge. It was strange at work; one day I'm there, married with two kids and the next thing you know I'm living with a man. Everyone at work was really good, although there were a few people who didn't understand. All my friends stuck by me. I didn't have a hard time with that like a lot of people do.

My wife and I get on fabulously. We've got two grandsons now. My new partner and I have been together for five years now and my little grandson asked, 'why don't you get married?'. Paul said, 'we can't get married, because of the laws in Australia'. My grandson said ,'I'll tell you what you do. You put a dress on and some lipstick and you two can get married and they'll never know'.

My new partner has got me into drag. If you said to me five years ago that he'd have me doing drag at the local theatre here, I would have laughed in your face. He's just very creative, he makes all the costumes so I get up there and perform. I invite all my work colleagues along and they love it.

I think things would have been much different if I'd had to go there (Vietnam) but I ended up joining the CMF. We call them the 'Weekend Warriors' where you had to do weekend service or something so you didn't go to Vietnam. But my father was dead against the war and he would have got me out somehow anyway. As a doctor he said, 'you're not going there, it's a useless war'. A few of my friends went. Other than that I just continued on.

I used to watch Mardi Gras and I love Mardi Gras and I actually went. I saw it a few times and then in 2007 I marched with the Surf Lifesavers. I'm a life member with Surf Lifesavers and everyone there knows I go down to Sydney for Mardi Gras and march, so I have represented Queensland for the last ten years carrying the flag. You will see me carrying the flag amongst the Surf Lifesavers and I tell everyone at work that I'm going down there and I'm really proud of that and I'm proud of how they have accepted it into the Surf Lifesaving movement.

My partner before this one ended up dying of the triple-A (abdominal aortic aneurism) unexpectedly.

He went to hospital one day and four days later I was turning off his life support. That was a massive thing for me. And because he was still technically married, his wife tried to get everything out of him. We went to court and she said, 'it's not a real relationship' and the judge was like Judge Judy and just scorned at her: 'You don't talk like that because one out of three ordinary marriages don't last and you're saying this is not a real relationship'. So she really stuck up for gay rights in the court that day and I was so proud of this woman for doing that. Actually I got him to go to Mardi Gras, which I never thought he would do. He was a manager in a really highflying company and unable to come out. I was so glad that he came out before he died so he could go to, I hate to say it, to his deathbed with the truth out. I got him to tell his brothers and sisters and his family knew and it was one of the best things I ever did, so he didn't die without being who he really was and being true to himself. I think I was put on this earth to do that with this man.

We'd met online, as you do. I don't like going to pubs and all that sort of stuff. It would have been a very long relationship, we bought a unit together. He was a really hard worker and everything. When you get older it's hard to find genuine nice people, especially through dating sites because people just lie and use fake pictures. There's just a lot of stuff that people do that's not right and that's why I'm open with people so they can take me as I am. I don't lie, I don't like it.

Gabby

I was offended at the bureaucratic system in South Australia the day they stopped doing gender reassignment surgeries at Flinders. that was something that affected me in South Australia. The system here couldn't help me, there's nothing in South Australia that could help me get anywhere. I found that frustrating and annoying. There were the problems with the doctor when he was misgendering me, he didn't get facts and figures correct, and he sent a letter to my doctor to try and hinder me getting hormone therapy. I found that to be the most disgusting thing a doctor or a professional could do. From that point on I decided the South Australian system can kiss my arse, and I would use whatever resources I could, so I got on the computer and found a gender specialist overseas.

I did my gender therapy via Skype from the comfort of my own home. My new specialist seemed to me more real than any psychiatrist did because he would ring me and talk to me on the spot. So he might call at two o'clock in the morning and I might be really pissed after a night out but I still had to take the call as part of the agreement. Whenever he called me I had to take that call. So he got to see me in a very raw, absolutely drunken state, but he really knew who I was. He was quite happy to give me my paperwork.

I had my surgery outside Australia. In Australia, surgery was still a two-stage procedure and it's a long, lengthy process to get the surgery. In Thailand it was a three and a half hour operation and that's it. After that operation I had a vagina, I had a clitoris, I had an inner and outer labia, I had it all. It's not a two-step procedure. In some places like America they take off everything and you'll have a clitoris with a catheter for a while and then they go back later and do the reconstruction of the vagina. In some places it's done in reverse, they'll do the vagina first and then the clitoris later. Europe and Thailand have more advanced surgery than places, simple as that.

Some people just don't trust going overseas and going overseas to have the operation comes with risks. The risks aren't necessarily the operation itself. The risks are after because you've got to travel back, so you're not resting. I was cramped up in an economy seat for nearly fifteen hours altogether in flight time and that was only fourteen days after the operation. I couldn't do anything. I couldn't do dilating and I couldn't do hygiene. That creates problems because the first few months after surgery are a delicate stage, and mine wasn't smooth running. I mean it was peak summer and I was sweating like crazy.

The first time my stitches ruptured was in Thailand, and that was due to a multiple combination of things. Because it's cosmetic surgery they use a fine thread to reduce scarring. But the fine thread couldn't take the heat and temperature, and so that broke probably five times. Then I had the rupture which was devastating. My vagina was a mess. It was truly terrifying. I mean, my blood pressure went up to a hundred and ninety-five and I had to race myself off to the hospital thinking I'm going to die, or worse, lose my vagina. But the doctor was calm and just said, 'Nah it's fine, it does happen'. It happens in one in twenty-five thousand girls, but that was unnerving. Afterwards then there was the trauma of not being able to dilate, that was a worry. I couldn't use normal dilation because of the rupture. I used a candle that they use for churches. I shaved the end to make it all nice and round and that was my first dilator. I was freaked out. I didn't let it affect me. It took me back a step and it threw my recovery plan and touring out the window because I was stuck in a hotel room. I couldn't go off touring or doing what I wanted to do. That's why when I was away back in 2015 I went ballistic. I rode two lots of elephants, I cuddled two lots of tigers, I watched monkey shows, crocodile shows, I did everything. It knocked me and threw out my schedule but it didn't throw me out.

I had a stitch burst so I had to get stitched up a few times. I ruptured myself and split my vagina in half basically and then I about a month later I got two haematomas and they nearly killed me. If they hadn't found the second one on the operating table I probably wouldn't be here today because I would have had septicaemia. But it was worth it and I'd do it again in a heartbeat. There's no way I wouldn't have done it, even knowing all those risks because I'm just happy with how I am now. I'm not ruled by something that's between my legs. It doesn't wake me up in the mornings. The only thing I miss about being a man is that you have to squat to go to the toilet but that's about it.

Philip

I think legislation has gone through as well as I could have expected, because we have a strong religious element working in our parliaments that is not necessarily reflected in the electorates, but it's certainly pushed upon our parliamentarians that they have to pass legislation that isn't upsetting to various religious groups. So, I'd say one of the major successes we've had in our parliamentary system is what we've been able to get through in spite of that. Now we have that legislation that would determine people to be in a partnership once they've lived together for a certain number of years. Then if they separate from each other and that goes to a law court, the court will assume that both people in the partnership have contributed. That's a big success, not just in terms of gay people. For example, across the road many years ago, there used to be two sisters living together. You could imagine if the older sister had the house in her name and wanted to take everything, then she could, or just give it to the cats' home, and the younger sister could be left completely bereft. Whereas that legislation changed it for the benefit of everybody. I like that sort of legislation, that isn't particularly directed just at gay people, but is directed at, and makes it better for, everybody in society.

That legislation meant that we've been able to organise our affairs, so we now have what we consider the same legal rights as to make us equal to any other couple in the street. We're quite happy, when we talk together about it, we're both quite happy with what we've been able to arrange.

Some people may then ask the question what if we were able to get married? My own feeling is that I would begrudge paying this government money for a licence to be married. I would begrudge that money. It's not about the marriage itself, it's about the money I would have to pay to this government to give me a certificate to say that I'm married. No way! If they gave me the certificate for free, oh yeah I'd be in it, but I'm not going to pay them any more money than I have to. The current legislation gives me the rights I need to carry on for what I want to do, without going through to get married.

Having said that though, we had a wonderful opportunity with the Feast Festival one year in 2007, where they had a guy who wanted to run a Loved Up ceremony, and that meant fourteen couples could exchange vows with each other. We had it at Montefiore Hill and a big ceremony there and a large reception over at Carclew.

That gave us a chance to invite a hundred of our friends and relatives to a huge ceremony and a huge celebration and that suited us perfectly, so they could all see that we were together. That's what mattered to us. Paying money to the government to get a certificate doesn't matter, in fact I totally don't want to do that. That was our high point, that opportunity to have a big commitment ceremony and have people who counted for us to come and see.

It's worthwhile being open about who you are, it's worthwhile taking some time to reflect and decide who it is that you are and not be wishy-washy about it. To be really quite strong about who you are, and of course there are going to be people who don't like it. Okay, so what? Of course there are always going to be people who oppose you, even if you're going to be wishy-washy. If you want to be everybody's friend, that's not going to work either. You just can't be everybody's friend. You've got to decide. We've had this discussion, Hugh and I, a few times when he wanted to say, 'We'd better not do this, or so and so might get upset'. And I'd say, 'It's us, it's about us. We're the ones that matter, they don't matter'.

I'm pretty happy with the way things are going and the way they've turned out. I'd like to think Hugh's got another ten, fifteen years, I'd like to think that. That would be a nice thing if it happens.

Gabby

My past is my past. I don't regret anything I've done but I use my past as a history to help others from my own experiences, and that's what I've done. I've helped conservatively tens of thousands of girls with my transition, conservatively, just knowing how to do things, what I did and what I shared. I know that I've done that. The emails and messages on Facebook and YouTube and even hearing when I've gone to Thailand. I had that fallout with the doctor, even before that point every single client that was going to his clinic and girls going see other clinics have all seen Gabby's video. To know that, that my videos helped so many girls have a more clearer picture and better understanding of what's ahead and not having that fear and anxiety. It's achieved exactly what it's meant to achieve. Even though I put it up just to share and have a memory and then maybe help one or two girlfriends, it's done so much more than that, it has helped thousands of people worldwide. It's my biggest achievement, I think. I've been astounded that in June 2015 it was struggling to get over a quarter of a million views. Now it's 1,600,000, which is 1,350,000 more views in two years. It seems to have slowed down now but it will probably spike again, it does that.

My first six months of transition from November 2010 into 2011 was a private time. I didn't tell anyone. If

I did it wasn't a big issue, just a minor conversation. I was transitioning internally. I would wear different layers of clothing so when I went outside people thought I was big and bulky. On August 27 2011 I came out publicly. I came out fully and told every single person that I knew right when I ran into them or whatever. Conservatively I'd estimate that ninety-six percent of all friends and family just walked away. A lot of mates just walked away. On top of that a lot of women complained that now they wouldn't be able to have sex with me. Why didn't they ask beforehand? Things like that I found quite amazing. I've got a best girlfriend now, Tracy. When I was Gary she never spoke to me. She never had anything to do with me because I seemed like a misogynous, Casanova type; I'd hit on women quite easily. But the day, and I mean the very day, I told her that I'm transitioning, she became my best girlfriend and new has lots to do with me. It's quite weird.

Over time the way people acted towards me slowly and gradually changed. At first when I transitioned I copped a lot of flak, covertly or through Facebook, or sometimes to my face. I had a couple of people come and give me shit to my face and they ended up on their arse pretty quick. One because he hit me and I just dropped him straightaway. I'm a very strong person. I can look after myself. Straight after hitting him police came in. Everybody knew him there and everybody knew who I was. I grew up here and I've been out in this area all my life, everyone knows me.

Even back in the day, I knew some people who would come to the nightclub and try to get in when they recognised me. But I'd tell them 'nah, I don't like you, get lost' (laughter). It was quite interesting. Suddenly they turn eighteen, or maybe seventeen, and come into town to try to get into a nightclub and the person they didn't want to run into was the person on the door.

I don't accept misgendering and not from anybody. I will correct them no matter who they are or where they are. I don't accept discrimination. If you're going to discriminate against me or treat me non-professionally then you are going to cop it and if you do it the wrong way and don't react the right way, you're going to cop something you didn't realise. Suddenly you're going to have not just this woman but this raging transgender woman screaming you to hell. I have had my time when I've given it back but I don't accept misgendering and I don't accept it for the simple reason that because I've gone, I believe I've earned my rights. I've paid for my rights and I've earned my rights so there's no way anyone should be misgendering me. I have breasts, I look like a woman. I may have very masculine characteristics but I'm a woman and they'll treat me as such. If you're going to misgender me then you are going to misgender the wrong person because I'm going to rip the shit out of you and I'm going to do it in public, I don't care.

I hate the word 'guy' or 'guys' that gets used so much. I'm not a guy, I'm a woman and don't disrespect me, simple as that. I'm a woman. You can me madam, you can call me miss, you can call me bitch, you can call me anything other you want to but don't call me by male terminology. I will not accept it. I have not gone all this way and fought for the rights I have to be accepting of that. I don't need to. My mum says to just ignore it, but why? Just because they're too bloody lazy to get their shit together why do I have to wipe their arse? They're small little things, they seem naïve, or not harmful, but it is. It's repetitive, it accumulates and when they start with one, they then start with two and if you let them get away with one little misgender suddenly they will do it again and again, and then other people hear it and misgender you too. So if you don't correct the one, then suddenly you are going to have a bigger problem, it becomes commonplace. So you've got to correct it. I'm very well-known. You can go into any shop up there and everyone will tell you who Gabby is. Not one of them would be likely to not know who I am. Everybody knows who I am around here. Most businesses around here know who I am—the big transgender bitch.

The benefits I've found being in the area and transitioning have been not so much for myself. It has been with the youth. I have noticed in the last four years, because of me transitioning so openly, so in-your-face and in this area. The bodies in the barrels case happened just down the road. I knew the victims, and I knew of those murderers too. So did everyone else here, that's what it's like to live in such a small community. So all these people see me transitioning here and transitioning so openly, which has helped other kids come out and it's helped parents who have their kids covertly transition be more proud and be more able to come out because they've seen someone else who is prepared to do it. There are more trans women out here now than there's ever been. I wasn't the first in the area. There was another one, Debbie, who used to be a bus driver. A friend of the family came out afterwards, Christine, but she is not my idol or the image of what I would like to be. She's got a vagina but has never used it in twenty-five years, so why the hell would you get one if you are not going to use it?

Me transitioning here has helped many others and others have transitioned out here over the years, on different paths, but not so publicly. They've transitioned in their home. I've been very, very open. People see me all the time and everybody knows who I am. So they knew Gary, they knew what Gary was about and suddenly it's like a big gossip session. It's like a grapevine. I know it has helped other kids. Even if someone chooses not to transition, seeing my experience has given them more scope to be who they are. They've been able to wear that pink shirt, that pink top, I see it's done that.

I very rarely even get kids who ask, but once in a blue moon I'll have a little child, under say seven or eight years, say to me, 'Are you a man or woman?'. My first response is that I'm a woman but I used to be a man. I don't hide it because it's not my responsibility to hide it, it's the responsibility of parents to educate their child correctly and properly. So I embarrass the parent because nine times out of ten the child's only said it because the parents raised it thirty seconds beforehand. Otherwise the child wouldn't ask that question straight out, the only reason they would ask that is because of their parents. Children will always bust parents. They will just come out with something similar to what they've heard. When I was younger I was in a relationship with a woman for a short period of time, and I asked her son one time where she was and he said, 'she's home in bed. She's lying in bed with Phil'. Her son just told me my girlfriend was lying in bed with another man. Kids will bust you, if you know what I mean. The best logic you can have for kids is complete honesty, if you try and snowball a kid they pick it. My nephews and nieces, even though some don't like me now, their kids are great and they adore Auntie Gabby. They all know that I used to be a man, they don't care.

David H

I auditioned for ABC radio at one point and I didn't get in. I think I opened my mouth and said something they didn't like. I did twenty-two years broadcasting at 3MBS in Melbourne. That was a major thing for me because I did just about every program. I did a lot of interviews and met some really top-notch musical performers from overseas. The way that I worked was if I had a musical guest come in—say Leslie Howard (pianist)—I would read up on them so that I knew enough and the questions would come out of that. It's very interesting that when you're interviewing someone and they realise you know what you're talking about, they tend to open up that and think, 'oh he gets it, he's not just someone talking to me because they have to'. There were some real good interviews that came out of it. I only stopped because they moved to somewhere that was very inaccessible by public transport and I thought I couldn't do it anymore.

Through my work in radio I've gotten to talk to the Melbourne Symphony Orchestra for several seasons, which was really good. I was actually gonged by the Hungarian government, because Franz Liszt was of particular interest to me and I did some programs on the centenary of his death and the Franz Liszt 2011 Bicentennial. The Hungarians decided to give six awards in Australia, which were specially commissioned bronze, and I was one of the six recipients alongside people like Leonard Burnside. It was a big deal and that is probably one of the few exterior acknowledgements that I've received out of all the musical stuff that I've done. It was a foreign country rather than my own country saying what you're doing is terrific and wanting to acknowledge that. I find that a paradox, really: the Hungarians appreciated what I did but I don't know whether the locals did or not. I found out later that a woman I knew who ran a musical interest group put my name forward to the Hungarian Embassy in Canberra.

There was a bias in my family against being a musician. There was a remark made about by mother saying musicians are all crazy why would anyone want to do that. That meant I had to rely on myself to recognise that music is what I wanted to do and have the resolve to follow through. I actually remember choosing, deciding that music is what I'm good at, so I went and got stuck into it. Also writing, in particular the Hartley thing which also involved music, was a means of me finding out who I was and what I could do. I've always loved words; I love crosswords, I'm articulate. My ex, who I split up with after ten years just a year ago, would complain at times that he'd never heard of a word I used, but I decided I'm not going to censor myself. If I use a big word, this thing is called a fucking dictionary and you can look it up. I had to recognise that okay I'm articulate, I'm nerdy whatever you want to say, a brainiac. I'm very musical and literate. I shouldn't have to dumb that down to fit in anywhere. I've deliberately made a decision that this is me, this is who I am. It's a matter of finding people who appreciate that and people who love me for who I am rather than trying to pretend or talk about football just to fit in somewhere. I'm not going to do that.

Mahamati

Anyway, I went to Cairns and sort of said goodbye to Adelaide for a while and the woman I was involved with. It was open ended; I left in May and we said we'd see where we were by Christmas and discuss. I was leaving because she had actually become violent and that was the absolute bottom line for me. She threw something at me and it bounced and hit me and I was quite badly hurt. I had to go to hospital and have my eye stitched. The relationship was petering out anyway, but that was the absolute last straw. How could I possibly stay in a relationship like that after working in domestic violence and women's shelters? It wasn't good, it wasn't nice. I had made a police report because I wasn't sure what I was going to do and didn't know whether I would press charges or not or whether the violence would continue. I was just unsure so I thought I best go report it as a precaution so that it was documented, which came from my domestic violence training. I had done that before I went to Cairns. We were corresponding a bit, but she found the police report and was absolutely incensed about that. It ended not so nicely and I knew it would be difficult having been with her for some time at this point. Her past relationships have always ended badly with a complete cut-off 'you're dead to me' type stuff and that's certainly what it's been.

I was in Cairns for six years. That was good. There is a great gay environment and I had really good gay friends. I had a lesbian relationship while I was there that was sort of on and off for some of that time. There wasn't much lesbian stuff happening there, it was a more of a gay party scene there because a lot of gay men come up from Sydney and Brisbane to live in Cairns because they could afford to live much better there. And it's warmer, which is good for people with HIV. There were also good services, they had stunning medical staff. David Bradford, who had been head of Melbourne sexual health clinic through the HIV era, was the main registrar in Cairns so people were confident in getting good treatment. He was like a magnet. Sun and David Bradford, what more could you need? There was a big gay party scene but there wasn't so much for lesbians, and those lesbians who were around were more of the gay party group than the lesbian women that I knew. So I started a lesbian book club just for the sake of it to try and get lesbians together. People came out of the woodwork and we developed things from that. It was much more combined than what my gay and lesbian experience was in Adelaide. Bfriend was different in that there was social stuff for gays and lesbians but my own personal network of friendships was still very much lesbian and the lesbian dances and that sort of stuff and gay friendships were probably more separate from that. I did get to go to some of the gay bars and parties and stuff. I had a joint fiftieth birthday party with the woman I was with at Semaphore and we invited a huge mix of people from the gay community, including her friends, my lesbian friends and gay guys. But our personal socialising was more lesbian orientated. That was certainly different in Cairns and I had some very good friendships there. We'd have to go to Brisbane frequently for meetings with the AIDS Council and they had an office on the Sunshine Coast and other places in Brisbane. My area was Cairns and Far North Queensland, which was fantastic because I got to travel quite a lot and meet a lot of people in that time. When I was in Cairns the Human Rights Commission asked Kenton and I to do another manual for rural service providers and we did one called Not Round Here. It's still online and it hasn't dated that much. He was in Melbourne and I was in Cairns. He'd write during the day and I'd get it at night and I'd write my bit and we'd go back and forth. Anyway, we got the damn thing done, it seemed unbelievable. That got launched in Melbourne and the commissioner also gave us a bucket of money to do some training so I got to do various regional trips.

I got to know a lot of people in Cairns and one of the workers there was a woman named Amber. She and her father were working in PNG so we went up to PNG several times. At that time PNG people who could afford it were coming to Cairns for treatment, which was the nearest port of call before treatment was regularly available in PNG. It was pretty grim times. People would think they could afford to make the trip and pay for medication, but they'd go back home and sooner or later the money runs out. Kids had to go to school and people couldn't keep up the regime of the medication enough for it to be effective. There were some deaths that were really sad, and some in Cairns too.

After six years and another funding crisis I got a job in Sydney doing many of the Lesbian Health Projects at ACON. That was great. It's a familiar sort of environment, just much larger, and they'd revamped themselves from the AIDS Council of New South Wales into a separate healthcare establishment that dealt with HIV, but also worked with other same-sex attracted and trans people, although it was a little more minimal in those days. I did the Lesbian Health Project for two and a half years. I enjoyed that, I met a lot of the Sydney lesbians. It was good.

I knew eventually I would want to come back to Adelaide and it was the only time I didn't have a funding crisis to precipitate a move. I decided it was about time to come home. I'd been away for nearly ten years by this time so I applied and got a job at what was the Positive Living Centre here in Adelaide. It was part of the AIDS Council in the old days, there was the AIDS Council and the Positive Living Centre was in the back area, but they eventually became their own thing and got their own premises at Glandore. They had been providing more social welfare type services to the positive population. At that time there was also a women's HIV project running out of the North Adelaide Women's

Health Centre, it's now defunct. After a few years at the Positive Living Centre and again a lot of involvement with the gay population in particular, there was another funding issue or another change in direction that they were doing and I didn't have a job for a while. Then I got a job at the AIDS Council again doing client support work and we were finding that the Positive Living Centre's new direction was all about health promotion and that sort of engagement, which I felt wasn't going to work and ultimately it didn't, because people didn't really want that, they wanted one-to-one assistance with things and didn't really want to go to groups and things that they're over and done with. It had some usefulness for some people, but that large population of long-term positive gay men who are fairly impoverished after living on disability for a long period of time, what they needed was one-on-one work for, say, getting an air conditioner and getting a grant and things like that. The AIDS Council could see that this wasn't working terribly well so I had a job there for about eighteen months doing similar sorts of things. At that time the Red Ribbon and Bobby Goldsmith Fund was a bit more affluent and so we were able to get a bit of assistance to individual people for things like glasses and medication and a whole range of stuff.

That eventually came to an end and I thought that would mean retirement I guess, and started to think what else I might do. I can't remember what I did, not much anyway. At that time I was living at a big house in Glandore and I had a lot of international homestay students staying at different times, particularly from China, Japan, and Korea. That was a lot of fun. Then I decided it was about time I moved into the unit that I bought here and about the same time I got another job at the AIDS Council. I came out of retirement for a project they had called Positive Directions, and it really quite suited me. It was working with long-term HIV positive people who were the most affected and isolated. They got a grant from MAC Makeup that was quite substantial and the program had been set up before I got into it. The previous guy had left and the program was probably in its second year. The job involved training volunteers and connecting them with positive clients, things I've been doing for donkey's years. If they got on alright we'd organise an arrangement where the volunteer would regularly come around and take the client out for lunch or to a movie, and MAC paid for it. It was my job to support the volunteers to keep on with the program and make sure everyone was happy.

About a year into that the AIDS Council went defunct permanently despite all the efforts to save it, particularly from Ian Purcell. The chairman of the board installed himself as acting CEO, which caused quite a number of issues and eventually no more funding came from the health department. The AIDS Council went bankrupt and that was the end it, which had a huge impact and it all happened very abruptly and very quickly. There was a bit of a scramble to obtain things like its archives. The library had shifted down to the AIDS Council premises on Fullarton Road, which was still operating quite well, though not as well as its more familiar long-term home at Darling House. I think Jenny Scott has got the library housed in archives somewhere in the State Library where she works.

After that I guess I retired for real and started to do a few other things. I didn't really know what I wanted to do so I did a training course for teaching English to migrants and did that for a while. I was a home tutor for new arrivals as part of a program called Talk to Aussies at Adelaide Uni where they link up volunteers with students learning English, generally masters students, so they get some exposure to Australian culture. It was interesting. So many of the Chinese business students said some of the lectures are even in Chinese. There are no Australians in the courses and they present the lectures and tutorials in Mandarin, which is amazing. A couple of the girls I met remarked that without Australians in classes and tutorials and living in an all-Chinese household then they may as well be in China. The program tried to link them up so they had some Australian cultural experience. I then did communications training with the university again, this time with dental students who English wasn't their first language, working on their communication with dental patients as part of their course. But I still wasn't sure what I wanted to do and then along came a friend, actually the first woman I ever got involved with. We were still friends and she was going to do this filmmaking course at ACH aged care group, but the course didn't fit with her schedule as she had surgery coming up. She suggested that I do it instead and I had nothing better to do so I thought I may as well do it. It was this very straight ACH aged care environment and we were able to do a film in a week, and they took notice of our feedback so the next time they did it they had a much better much longer program. I wanted to do something that was a bit different so I did a story about a couple of lesbian friends of mine and their cats. It was a typical lesbian cat story so I did a little film about them and their cats and their lesbian relationship of twenty years. The film was shown at the Mercury and on their website and I felt a bit victorious in getting a bit of lesbian material included. It wasn't overtly non-gay friendly and there was nothing to suggest that it could be, it's just that there was nothing visibly queer and so I had a bit of a mission to have something be different.

By luck another gay friend I had known around the traps for a very long while also happened to do that course too just by an absolute fluke. He made a film on his volunteer work at the Hutt Street Centre and also about him being gay. He has a very interesting story, and he's written a really good book called *The Lacemaker's Son* about his gayness. He came from Estonia as a young man, and he was sold by his parents for a whiskey, or wine, or something like that, or schnapps when he was five. He ended up doing this course the same time as me so we had two gay films out of the six.

After I'd done the course I wondered what I was going to do next The AIDS Council was going to resurrect itself, but I didn't feel that at seventy I'd have any chance of getting a job. I didn't feel particularly fulfilled in the long-term with what I was doing with the teaching. It was okay but I wasn't madly drawn to it. I looked around for other film making. I'd always done some writing but I'd never considered film and I knew nothing about it. I found out about this course at MAPS at Hamilton High, so I went to an open night and applied. They get up to one hundred applications and they take thirty students. It's been going for over twenty years and they make thirty films for the first years. So I got to make three films the first year. I'd love to get the money to do the first film I made over again, it was a bit of a flop.

The thing to know about this course is the students are mostly eighteen- to nineteen-year-old kids who want to make films but don't want to go to university. The school works similarly to the film industry. You can pitch a film that you want to make and the class votes on it rather than the teachers. The kind of films I want to make is probably not want eighteen- and nineteen-year-olds want to make, as they want to make shootouts, forest chases, cars, stuff like that, not all of them but overall. When I got my chance to pitch I did a bit of lobbying to the other students. I wanted to make my film on a HIV-positive man who hides all the evidence of being gay from his caregiver, so when she comes over he puts away his porn and locks up his DVDs and suffers through her home visits. The idea was good but it flopped a bit and it was my fault in the direction that it flopped. It was my first film and I wasn't sure how much I could push it. It could have been saved with some good editing, but that didn't happen.

The next film I did was on narrative therapy, which is something I've been involved with over the years at the International Centre in Adelaide, and they do amazing work around the world and here. I wanted to do something on one of the aboriginal elders, including some of her story and some of her teaching narrative therapy. The third film I made was on my polio story and is probably the best of the three. I did interviews with a neurophysiologist who does a lot of physio work with post-polio patients, and bit of historical background. In second year the structure was a little bit different, you didn't have to pitch your idea and didn't depend on a class vote to get your film and you work on a documentary. I ended up making a documentary on the queer youth drop-in and did interviews with the kids. I was pleased to get that done. I had a second film in the wings that I didn't actually get to make. David, my ex-husband, was incredibly ill at the time and it looked like he might die. One of my sons was home from London and everything was just a mess for a couple of months. He eventually survived but it didn't look like he was going to. At the time I was supposed to be getting paperwork production done to get the film up and running, and I just couldn't get it done so I missed out on making the second film, but that's alright.

Michael

I don't know what else I would have done in life. I quite enjoyed teaching. Those were the days when teachers were expected and encouraged to teach, rather than being 'facilitators' for more child-centred learning, informed by the insights of the social sciences. I noticed in the last years of teaching, perhaps about 2003-04, that I came across a television trolley outside my classroom. A student had scrolled some graffiti identifying me as gay, and the following day another boy in response had written, 'So what? Get a life!'. This was a glimpse that perhaps by the early twenty-first century some attitudes were perhaps changing in the school culture. Not necessarily from some parents but certainly among the boys who had relatives or brothers at university. At an August formal organised by the prefects before the major exams, I was somewhat amazed to see some senior boys arriving with their female partners greeting each other with friendly hugs and occasional cheek kissing. It was a social change that I had been unaware of; a few boys were beginning to identify as gay at school. Staff were counselled on strategies to prevent bullying and harassment.

In pursuing my goals of education and travel, I have tended to be self-reliant and fairly independent. I have remained peripheral to gay advocacy campaigns, though in the 1990s I started attending workshops at Darling House and borrowing books from its excellent library. I've had the occasional personal relationship since then but based mainly on friendship and social activities.

Throughout my professional career I remained largely discreet and prudent, and tended to ignore the elements of homophobia if and when they appeared. As for my private life, I have retained an optimistic view of life, which has been an asset when confronting the health challenges of ageing. I don't feel strongly about same-sex marriage but I will support it as a rights issue. I am attracted to the French practice where marriage is a civil rite and couples may follow it with a religious ceremony without any legal status.

Because I have been trained to question moral absolutes based on ancient 'scriptures', I regard myself as an atheist now. In the 2016 census I identified myself as atheist and 2011 as animist. I'm interested in religion intellectually, because I think what one believes about the divine often shapes the way one lives. I don't regret having spent those years deep in theology. I don't have a religious belief. An understanding of religion is essential for understanding politics by and large. I like to see a fair and just society. The good things that we have in Australia were legislated, such as a basic minimum wage and Medicare. I'm a strong supporter of multicultural society and the immigration of skilled migrants. I think those dreadful days of police harassment of gays were terrible, but they much reflected the mores and prejudices of a conservative society. I think the police force has changed to a certain extent. Actually, I toured SA Police Academy in 2016 with a seniors group and saw the trainees, mainly men. I'm sure they were told to say polite things to us and it is encouraging that they're getting a better education. But I didn't see a lot of non-Caucasian faces amongst the cohort, especially Asian, which I found disturbing.

I would like to see philanthropic enterprises offering means tested scholarships for young Australian in their twenties to be able to travel overseas temporarily to experience different cultures, especially to get them out of Adelaide or Australia. Today most are encumbered by HECS debts.

Thomas

I don't really remember setting any goals. Some people might but I didn't set any goals. I just lived my life. I just wanted to be happy and healthy and I think those goals are still the same. Probably my most satisfying achievement was having the two kids, who are absolutely loved. I've done a lot of sport. I competed in two marathons and eleven half marathons. I competed in about two hundred triathlons and I've cycled from Brisbane to Sydney. And marching with Surf Lifesavers for ten years at Mardi Gras is a big thing for me as well, so that's one of my achievements. I found that just recently there is a place in Peregian Beach, a men's club, I was in there the other day and actually saw another guy that was doing triathlons with me and I didn't know he was gay. They're out there, they're everywhere. I don't like people who class people, that's another thing I hate. I think it's so wrong to put someone into a category. We're all different, we're all born individuals.

I got into sport when I was really young but fell out of it when I had kids, and then I got back into sport in my early forties. If I want to relieve frustration and stuff, I get on my bike and clear my mind. If I'm upset or unhappy I just go harder to get rid of all the doubts, so that's the way I deal with my stresses in life. I've got a small group of friends who I'll go out with, and they all know my sexuality so that's fine. I've got male and female straight friends that are fine with it. A lot of people I know who do triathlons, that's all they talk about, that's who they are, and people get sick of that after a while. You got to have a good mix, you've got to have a life.

They say age is wisdom and I really think it is. You change your attitude and it's not all about going fast anymore it's about doing things that are important and meaningful to you. I overcame my problems by setting goals, working hard, and training hard. I get up at four in the morning and go riding before work and people ask why I do it, but if I had a race or something to train for nobody would think twice about it. My greatest supporters over the years have been my various partners, because they've had to give up a lot to take me to races, going here and there, even when they're not really into it. Before John died I got him to try cycling and he was really going quite well before he got sick. I think it changed his life in that respect, because I kept trying to keep him fit and everything.

I got him to Mardi Gras, which I'm just so proud of because he had to hide a lot from his friends and family and he was in very high profile job in Brisbane. He asked me if he should tell his boss, and I told him it was up to him, but there's still that worry of how it might affect your career. He also was a teacher in a boys school at one stage and I thought if they knew that he was gay he probably would have lost his job over that. It's just the way society is. I think it was daunting for him because even though he was a good teacher if they knew his sexuality they just wouldn't accept it, that's just how they work up here, it's still outback Queensland. There's still a long way to go and they all say we're equal but they're not in certain parts.

I find it's much more accepting in Sydney and Melbourne, even in Adelaide. I've got a cousin who is married in Adelaide. They had a big ceremony (Loved Up) there where probably twelve couples got married. I don't think the laws were changed then, it was a while back. I went down for his wedding and I keep in touch with him still. But up here there's no way I would walk down the street holding hands or anything, it's just still very backwards up here. That's just the way it is.

The main thing there should be more love, more peace and more acceptance of what and who people are, and stop judging people, putting them in different categories. Let them be who they are as long as they're not hurting anyone else. More trust and more forgiveness. Even if gay marriage came in straight away I don't know if I would do that, but I'd love to see it for others, it's just their whole dream and everything. Our relationships just don't get accepted. They say we're equal but if I was to get my partner to move in with me now they would probably cut the pension from me even though we're not husband and wife, you know what I mean. When it suits the government to recognise your relationship so they can cut your pensions they will, but they won't let you go and get married, and that sort of stuff I think is wrong.

I think I'd like to make that commitment (moving in) with my partner. He's lived in Adelaide and has always been gay and never had lots of partners. He's the most beautiful person and this is the longest relationship he has ever had. We get along so well together. It's all to do with trust. If he does something I just ask him to tell me about it, which is just part of how our relationship works. We don't hide anything from each other, so if he wants to go into a sauna and muck around

I just want him to be careful and have fun. I don't put restraints on him.

I think the most important lesson is to not judge. People have feelings and most people are doing the best they can, you don't know what other people are going through. Even though I try not to I find that I judge people I work with. These are people who've had strokes and broken hips and I go to their houses and their living conditions aren't great. So I just put myself in their shoes and think about what these people have gone through. You tell yourself she's old and she's got one tooth, but you don't know she's going through hell and she held her partner in her arms while he died. But people just judge and they don't know that everyone has their own things going on in their lives so try to be more tolerant. I'm trying to be more tolerant these days.

2010s

The ACT Legalises Same-Sex Marriage
For less than a week in 2013 same-sex marriage was legal in the Australian Capital Territory. The law passed the territory parliament but was immediately challenged by the Abbott Liberal Government as the first priority issue that they took to the High Court.[21] This occurred whilst the Prime Minister and other Liberal spokespeople consistently denied that same-sex marriage was an important issue for the government. The court ruled that the Federal Government had the right to decide marriage laws in the country and any state law would be overridden by the Federal Marriage Act.

Adoption, Gender Identity and Surrogacy Laws Passed
In February 2017 it became legal for same-sex couples to adopt in every Australian jurisdiction. South Australia was the last to amend its laws, despite the fact that decades before it lead the way on equalising the law for LGBTIQ people and couples.[22] The last of the laws passed when a UK same-sex couple with two adoptive children were caught up in the South Australian

bureaucracy, which didn't have a system for processing 'non-traditional families' who migrate to Australia. After years of lobbying and petitioning the laws passed in South Australia, bringing it in line with the rest of the country.

The Turnbull Government Creates a Same-Sex Marriage Postal Survey

Over many years and two Liberal Prime Ministers, the government continually passed off same-sex marriage as a low importance issue. Despite this, the topic dogged the coalition government and forced several long meetings of the party to focus on this single issue over every other policy and legislative concern. Prime Minister Tony Abbott proposed a compulsory plebiscite as a means of taking action without taking a position on the issue. Once he was deposed, his successor Malcolm Turnbull failed to pass the plebiscite in the Senate, facing opposition as the plebiscite was deemed unnecessary due to known broad public support for same-sex marriage and it absolved the government of its responsibility to legislate. Instead Turnbull decided to push the issue onto the Australian people through a non-compulsory postal survey, the first of its kind since 1998.

On 15th November 2017, the Australian Statistician chief of the ABS David Kalisch announced the outcome of a three-month-long postal survey that asked Australians 'Should the law be changed to allow same-sex couples to marry?'.[23] Sixty-one point six percent of Australians who voted said yes while thirty-eight point four percent voted no. The significant result saw all states and territories return a majority yes vote and put the issue back into the hands of politicians.

David D

In the past, Melbourne was very conservative but had amazing nightlife. There was Club 80 in Melbourne, I had a very wild life at Club 80. Darwin was very small but they had a sex on premises site at a sex shop called Fantasy Lane. You paid five dollars to go through the doors and they had glory holes and things, but it was very tacky because there was no running water and they had TV screens playing porn. I had a bit of fun there, but Darwin had a very small nightlife. Adelaide is in between, I feel like I'm out of the rat race of Melbourne but I can easily go to Melbourne on a plane. Both my sisters are over there, Dorothy died last June but Val is still alive and I am very close to her. They were both smokers and Val had one lung removed with cancer about seven year ago and when she gets the all clear from the oncologist every six months, she's off overseas like a Bondi Tram. All three of us have always known how to enjoy life.

Australia has come a long way in openly showing the individuality of sexuality on television and how it is wrong to place labels on ourselves. We need to be open and honest about who we are. We need marriage equality. We should never forget that homosexuality was once illegal, there was criminal imprisonment, police entrapment, bashings and murders. I was once bashed by two policemen and immediately suffered a mental breakdown because of it. We must remember those who have suffered and died from HIV/AIDS and the stigma that was attached. Gay men can be very cruel with ageism and the pursuit of the young body beautiful. Old age can be lonely at times. I live in an ECH (Enabling Confidence at Home) life interest unit near a tram stop in Glenelg. I gain great strength from my membership with the Pilgrim Uniting Church, which is strong in acceptance of sexuality and urban mission. Also the Adelaide Gay and Lesbian Qwire and the Glenelg Community Centre for many games of Scrabble. My biggest wish is for people to embrace socialising with grace, empathy and good humour.

David H

In May last year (2016) the Premier had an afternoon in State Parliament where various politicians and different parties spoke and he invited gay men who had been prosecuted back in the seventies and eighties, some of whom were there. The idea was to do a state apology to gay men who had been caught up or imprisoned or had gone overseas because of the scandal. The speeches went on for about an hour. As I was sitting there in Queens Hall my mind was just reflecting and I was suddenly aware of something that happened when I was around twenty. This was literally fifty years ago if not a couple more and it just fell into my consciousness. I was actually a bit stunned. I think it came from hearing some of the stories from the gay men who were mentioned by the Premier, things that had happened to them, it just sort of flicked up.

When I was first getting sexually active I got onto some guy. I can't remember all the details. I was living with my parents at the time and he use to come drive close to the house and I would go out to meet him and then we would go back to his place or whatever. We were in the car driving along a major highway in Melbourne and the police pulled us over. This was before cars had seatbelts, so the reason was that we were sitting too close together in the front seat of the car. I may have had a hand on his leg (I honestly can't remember) so we were obviously close. The police called us out individually to quiz us and I overheard the police ask him my surname and I made sure I knew his. Luckily I've got a very calm exterior so neither of us got flustered, because I think if we did and we let something slip they would have taken us back and charged us or arrested us or bashed us or something. I thought then that it's incredible that something like that could have happened only fifty years ago. They wouldn't get away with it these days so that rather astonished me that I actually had forgotten that memory.

Hugh

So, who are the most significant people in my life? My mother, of course, because she was a musician too. Also she gave me unconditional love. My English teacher at high school because he taught us logical thinking, which was way ahead of his time. He was an extraordinary man and he also taught us from texts that at the time were hot off the press. For instance, he got us to read Christopher Fry's play, *The Lady's Not For Burning*, which had just been produced in London and which I later performed in at university. And Philip is a major, major influence in my life in almost every way, and gives me practical and emotional support. He's also taught me many new things, especially financial responsibility, because before I met him I was drifting. I was a late developer about money. He's also given me amazing love and joy for thirty-three years.

What have I learnt from all that? I've learnt that self-hatred and guilt are terribly destructive things and can lead to dreadful things like suicide. That the most important thing in life is to accept yourself as you are. That logical discussion and critical thinking are incredibly important in a civilised society in order to keep people civil, rather than just abusing people who don't agree with you and calling them scumbags. I would like to see people attain those things and so attain their full possibilities. I'd like to see more protection and counselling for those in need, especially for young people, but also older people.

We've seen lots of older men, especially coming out of failed marriages, who are in despair. I know we seem like a stable couple. We actually have lots of ups and downs like any couple, but people like to think of us as a shoulder to weep on and we hear lots of stories. Sometimes it's enough just to listen.

I'd like to see an end to violence and bullying especially in schools. I had some of that when I was a lonely and miserable adolescent, and I'll never, ever go near that school again.

And that's about it.

Gabby

What we're missing in this country right now is for our government to get off their arse and that's all politicians. They need to take the religious philosophies and ideologies out of all this crap of transition medicine and allow people to freely transition with help from the government. Even if it costs money, because it saves money.

What the government will spend on a transition, which may cost forty to fifty grand in that initial phase, would save them hundreds of thousands of dollars in mental health over twice as long a period because you only have to look at each time you go to a psychiatrist. It's a scam, you go in and you pay eighty or seventy dollars to them but they're getting three hundred and fifty dollars from the government. Those psychiatrist appointments are compulsory, they want eleven visits and that adds up to a huge amount of money, and it doesn't need to be. That money is a third of what it costs for someone to have a sex change. Or the cost of their hormones for three to five years. It's stupidity and the government needs to wake up in that respect and understand it fully, and it just needs to let the system work in the right manner as it does anywhere else internationally. It's stupidity that our system is so advanced in some areas, like having feminine identity markers on our paperwork and yet we are behind in surgery, we're behind in the care that you need to transition. Kids in Australia are only just now getting the care that they should have got years ago. The rise in the numbers of cases going into Monash for gender dysphoria has risen astronomically in the last few years.

That massive increase is because over the last six years transgender people have not had to hide anymore. Suddenly transgender issues are becoming visible, people are seeing that trans people are around, some phobias are starting to go away, because of the people who have come out. And our government, like America, is going backwards. America was leading us in transgender rights but now it's started going backwards. Unless you've got the money to do transition, you're going to have a shit hard time, especially in South Australia or anywhere in Australia.

Even if you've got money to get your transition you are still going to have a shit time, because there's no help. You'll get discounts on your hormones, but that's it. If you've got to have surgery here in Australia you are looking at close to twenty-six thousand dollars to have a sex change, minimum. If you go to Thailand the cost is closer to eleven thousand dollars, unless you want to be really risky and go to the office clinics and pay only two thousand dollars, though I don't know how you're going to end up at the end of it. Learning through my own experience of transition I've worked with a number of girls who have done their transition that way, Asian girls, and I've spent hours on Skype showing them how to clean themselves after surgery because not all the information is out there. I'd be naked myself to show them how to do it because of translation problems. There are some very, very shoddy places over there. There are some good ones too. There's a brilliant clinic that can do the whole process, it's a lot more costly, but you go through all the different sides of it. People don't just go to Thailand for the surgery, they go for the experience because each girl who goes to Thailand brings a bit of Thailand back with them. Most girls I know who have been to Thailand have a fondness and love for Thailand.

Our governments are creating problems for themselves because they increase the costs. If my surgery was done here to the same standard that it was done in Thailand, I wouldn't have had my problems, because I wouldn't have been flying. Girls will be taking risks going overseas to other doctors and then having to come back home without having post-op care, and then the Australian system has to look after them. The Australian health system has to clean up the mess from that doctor or the post-operative care they just couldn't get because they had to leave Thailand to come home.

The government can change the whole thing by removing a lot of barriers and impediments to gender issues and to marriage. I find it so stupid that as a man I could marry a woman and now that I'm a woman I can only marry a man, but I'm bisexual and I'm still attracted to women but I can't marry one. It's stupidity. I can marry a Thai ladyboy who looks everything like a woman and has even had the surgery, because the paperwork would still say male (they can't change gender markers in Thailand), but I can't marry a transgender girl from down the road or a woman. Our government creates bigger problems.

We're still making progress and I can't see us going backwards, except with the marriage act. We haven't moved forward enough to worry about going back, if you know I mean. If we were implementing our surgeries and doing the surgeries without all the red tape and then lost that, then that would be bad. If we suddenly stop giving therapy to these youths and young kids who are coming through transition I believe that would be detrimental, because then they would have live it how I lived it. They'd have to suppress themselves for so long, and that took me a lot of energy to hide my transgenderism. I would invest easily thirty percent of my daily energy suppressing or hiding. It's exhausting and that's what people don't understand about living in the closet with gender dysphoria, trans people have to battle it internally and even though they might not show it a lot of energy has been used. A lot of physical energy. The day I came out was huge relief, to know I didn't have to hide it and I was proud to say it. Even the day the prolactin kicked in and that thing didn't wake up in the morning with a massive rager, that was heaven. I knew it still worked, don't get me wrong, but it would wake me up every morning. I don't get that anymore. It used to distract me because I might see someone I like on TV and suddenly it rises. It takes physical energy to suppress it.

I think that more education is important to increase understanding. I found that every time I was in hospital, which has been eleven or twelve times since 2013, that the staff there were craving information. At one hospital I probably had thirty to forty nurses come into my room, all wanting to know and look and see what it's all about. When mum had cancer and I was visiting, nurses would ask information. There's not enough understanding within the medical field to know totally all about it and I'm telling doctors that I'm post-operative woman and they couldn't work it out. They didn't even know I was post-operative, when I've got my legs spread and I've got the haematomas and they didn't know I was a post-operative woman,. You'd think they'd be able to know straight away. I had to tell them. It was the same with the nurses. No vagina is exactly alike, every single one of them looks different, which is fortunate for transgender women because you can't tell by looking at it that it's not the original plumbing. Modern surgeries don't allow visual scarring. All my scarring is within my own labia, which you can't see so you can't tell that it's been made by a doctor. The only thing that gives me away is my voice. I have a deep voice, otherwise no one really has any idea, they just think I'm a really strong bitch.

If I had not been robbed of my inheritance from my previous lover's will I would have used the assets from that to achieve what I can achieve now. In other words, I am happy with who I am because I've done what I can within the constraints of my resources, in terms of money and time. But if I didn't have those constraints and had unlimited resources, then I would have altered my face even further. I probably wouldn't have altered my voice because I'm not one hundred percent happy with voice surgeries. The success rate is only seventy to eighty percent, which is not high enough for me and it would mean going to hospital instead of day surgery.

Mahamati

I think South Australia is particularly disadvantaged in that we don't have a very good uniting or communication system at all. We only have the one newspaper, *Blaze* (now defunct), that came out once a month and didn't contain much of relevance. I didn't know one lesbian who read it. Feast Festival happens only once a year, and that's getting in trouble with its internal politics. A lot of lesbians remain apart from it but an awful lot don't. We lack any real means of coming together or communicating as a group, so there's no community centre, we don't have a Mardi Gras, we don't have a Midsumma. Feast Festival here is much less than it used to be, there's a lot less community than it used to have.

Everybody wants the pink dollar and the grey dollar and most of them want it together, so all the aged care establishments are marketing towards the older LGBT community and trying to demonstrate visibility and that they're LGBT friendly. Some of them don't know what it means but others do and are working quite hard.

We don't have a uniting need. At Ian's funeral there was more people than I had seen in one place for years. The work that gay men had done with the Uranian Society, which has been such a great long-standing event for gay men and women, hasn't been sustained. I wonder if it's because we don't have that leadership.

We used to have so much stuff and now there's really nothing. Heavens, we don't need another HIV/AIDS crisis but now there's nothing to rally people together in order for anything else to happen.

It remains to be seen whether the younger ones coming up through the various youth programs run by MIFSA and SHineSA will be the sort of people who are innovators and community builders or not. I haven't seen much of that yet. There are some really competent young people out there but there's not the same employment possibilities where they can utilise. Second Story used to employ peer educators and there were lots of opportunities for volunteering at the AIDS Council and libraries where people could expand themselves, get educated and be exposed to different experiences.

Travis

It's sad and unfortunate that we are even having a debate about same-sex marriage. My own position would be to abolish marriage entirely but that's not really going to happen. I see the 'no' campaign, the anti-same-sex marriage campaign, as something driven not so much by religious belief, but as in a conservative movement clinging onto church support and power. In our supposedly secular society we have churches that are inordinately powerful and in marriage, for example, the churches do have the say at present that who can get married and who can't. I see it as them simply wanting to retain that power. I think one of the things we need to do is to separate church and state, which means more religious freedom, less power to the church, and then perhaps we'd see some transparency about who is making rules, who's running things.

This is not just queer society but society in general. We don't care enough about young people and we don't treat them well enough. We expect them to keep their rooms tidy but we don't actually give adolescents responsibility that I think they generally crave and would do well with, and then when we expect young people to stay hardened and expect them to look for a job and we tolerate a youth unemployment of twenty-five percent. So we tell them to work hard to get something that's not possible. I think we could do a lot more to make young people feel like they really are participants in our society.

AIDS (something to never forget). Australia did particularly well with AIDS if you look around the world. We did particularly well in containing the AIDS epidemic but we could have done better if we had been more open to honest discussion about sex, sexuality, drug use and the actual things that needed to be done to keep this epidemic under control. We're still way too sexually repressed, which doesn't necessarily mean saying we need to have more sex—that would really be an individual's call—but we could be a lot more open and honest about our own and others' sexuality and be a lot more accepting about what life is like for other people. If we did that it would be far less likely that something like the AIDS epidemic would get out of control because we would be able to identify there's a new STI going around and we need to get on top of that somehow. That would mean we could actually, as we've done with AIDS, target our interventions without using code. Instead, we could use pictures.

We can tell children about sex and be sure that they're getting information from good sources. Just as a little sideline, if children have the language around sex and sexuality they then have the capacity to speak up about what is happening to them that they don't like. Not teaching children about sex doesn't protect them, it just makes them vulnerable. So lessons learned, secrets cause us a lot of trouble and we should be cautious about keeping and perpetuating secrets.

That's the Netflix dilemma, when it comes to what I would want for the world if there were no limits. It used be that sitting home on a Sunday night there were only three movies on free-to-air television to choose from and that was all, so you just had to decide which of those three movies you wanted to watch. But now with Netflix you're faced with countless possibilities and can't decide. This is the difficulty I have what would I wish for. I suppose saying I want something wouldn't imply that I don't want other things. But what's really, really important?: freedom, openness, respect, allowing people to express who they are, and if we could do more to allow people to express who they are, and a bit less time judging and trying to suppress them.

David H

Carl was very good while we were together and we're still friends, he said if I ever need help he'd provide it. For example, I did some presentations playing live music to a whole lot of writers who all knew each other for Alliance Française here in Melbourne. I speak basic French and I love French culture so I did one of the presentations on Paris in the thirties and forties, and the other I did on Napoleon the Third and the rebuilding of Paris. I'm not technological by any means, and so Carl put a lot of work into creating a visual presentation on the computer using portraits, photographs and cartoons so there was a visual element as well, and I loved doing that. He insisted on doing it for my last concert as well. He would be there for me in the background just to support me and I really appreciated that, it took off the lonely edge. Even though I was the main focus, at least I knew I had support there. Then if anything technical went wrong he was there to sort it out while I went on with the show. It's very important for me to find people to collaborate with. When I was doing the radio I would script, program and present my show, and then they required me to do all my panelling work, answer the phone, and quite often to answer the fucking door.

I know a professional broadcaster who used to be on commercial radio here, and her eyes would just pop open at the thought of everything I had to do because she had a producer to manage everything. I look back and wonder how the hell I managed to do all that. No wonder I had that headache at the end of the show.

Because of my background I took a lot upon myself, and if you're a perfectionist you push yourself, but I've gotten better at saying I need help because of my piano concerts. I know how to do a lot of it myself but I also really need to be able to say I need some help. I'm getting better at that. I remember saying to myself that my standards are so high and if I just aim for eighty percent it's still going to be dammed good, so don't worry if it's not ninety-nine percent.

One thing that really has to change is arts funding and the attitude towards the arts. I remember there was an inquiry into arts funding quite some years ago now and there was an athlete on the investigative panel and she had the gall to say the arts have to get more popular to deserve more money and get more people involved. You just need to look at the number of people who go to galleries throughout the year compared to football attendances. She had missed the point entirely. Part of it comes to education in schools. When I was in secondary school there might have been one hour of music a week, which was listening to records or something and no music program. Now the school has a big fat fancy music school program. But there's still a lot of work to be done. A conductor based in Melbourne is pushing to get people into music education early and that's the only way to really improve that.

I think same-sex marriage will be a very defining moment, and the fact that a lot of young dudes just can't see what the problem is shows how far things have come from fifty years ago, from the experiences I started with. The police wouldn't get away with stopping a car and grilling two guys just because they were sitting close together now.

I was reading *The Age* about the situation on Manus Island, this whole horrendous thing of demonising people who come by boat. But then any number of people come here by plane and overstay their visa and nobody's bothered by it, probably because a lot of them are white. I'm deeply appalled by how that whole debate has become an absolute festering. I'm a little bit heartened that the Labor Party has made a statement about people on Manus and said it's got to be dealt with, because it's long overdue. I do worry about hardening attitudes and One Nation playing into the bias of certain groups of people. It's really appalling.

The importance of the apology in State Parliament was addressing that very thing. When I went through my archives recently I found an article on two men who were arrested in Collins Street Melbourne for kissing in a doorway. Their names and addresses were published. One was a university lecturer, a slightly older guy, and he had to go overseas to protect himself. The other one was a young unemployed guy living in the western suburbs of Melbourne. He was probably given a really hard time. We need to just reflect on the terrible suffering that was caused to gay men particularly through that whole period. A lot of it has changed for the better, and a lot of young people have no conception of the whole history there. Gay might be cool these days but it hasn't always been that way.

If I could wish for just one thing I think it comes down to use that much used word, love. If you love yourself then you can love somebody else, because you don't have that blocked air. I'm not Christian, but if we could return to the idea of accepting other people no matter what the differences, or at least try to meet them halfway, life would be a lot easier. because human beings whether they're dumping stuff on people of a different colour who are stuck on an island just trying to get to Australia, if we could just stop demonising people it would remove a lot of that angst people feel and we wouldn't be in a position we're in now. You only have to read the *Herald Sun* to see the ranting and raving that goes on in the letters page, because dumping on someone else might make them feel better about themselves for five seconds. Or there's Pauline Hanson, who's such an angry woman who just seems to need to find something to peg her anger on. I think she should just go away, get a therapist and work on herself. But it's never going to happen. Her quivering rage is all about her, and has nothing to do with the minority groups she dumps on.

Post

Phillip (P) and Hugh (H) Reflect on 33 Years Together

P: Oh that's an easy story. It would have been about 1983 and there was a gay bushwalking club called the Happy Wanderers. It's still around now, but I think back then it just called itself gay bushwalkers, didn't it?

H: No, no, it was the Happy Wanderers then too.

P: Hugh was the leader of one of the walks and I'd been thinking about going on such walks for quite a while, because if you're gay you have to go out and meet people, and there wasn't all that many other options to meet people.

H: He was very brave. He didn't know anybody in the group.

P: So the deal was that you meet at the house of a guy called Bart in North Adelaide before the walk and go from there. We went up to Para Wirra. I had never been on such a walk before and I thought you had to take everything with you, so I did. I took my best demi-tasse coffee cups and I took percolated coffee and apricots slices and a tablecloth. You have to have all the catering done, it has to be done right, because you could die of hunger out there. It's in the wilderness. You remember, when you went to school you learn that you could die through starvation in the wilderness? And I thought, 'That's not going to happen to me'.

H: Everybody else in the walking group took instant coffee and plastic mugs, but Phillip turns up with percolated coffee, with bone china cups and saucers.

P: Anyway, so that's where I met Hugh. He was the leader of the walk. Part of the walk was through a goldmine, so I like to think that he's my nugget of gold. (Hugh clasps Philip's hand) But immediately we were tested, because immediately after that you went on a study tour in Hungary.

H: I was in Hungary on a scholarship, which meant I was away for about three months.

P: He went to do his study, and then when he came back we just resumed as if we'd gone to bed that night and woken up the next day. I mean you could pine about things, I suppose that would be getting in the road of eating lamb curry. I'm not really the world's most emotional person when it comes to those deep emotions. I guess that was a bit of surprise for Hugh, wasn't it?

H: Uh huh.

P: Anyway. I was around when you got back and it just went on, as if you hadn't been away.

H: When I first saw Phillip I thought he was the most handsome man I had ever seen in my life, and I still think so. It was like as the French say '*le coup de foudre*', the bolt of lightning.

P: So after a bit, he put a trailer on the back of the car and we moved from the Temple and came here.

H: Because he'd been looking after the old monk in the Temple.

P: Because prior to that I'd ride my bicycle over and bring things here wouldn't I, while you were sitting here in the darkness?

H: My saviour. It didn't happen all that quickly. It wasn't until August that you moved in.

P: Because we had to find somebody else to move into the Temple. I started working for TAFE part-time and Hugh was still working for the ABC, but then that all got rather difficult. So after a few months he started working for TAFE as well.

H: We were very, very fortunate in our boss for part of that time. We started to work for a project called the Indonesian Polytechnic Project, and we had a wonderful boss who employed us both knowing that we were a gay couple, and supporting that and accepting that fully, so all the staff and the students did as well. This was really, really exceptional.

P: Yeah, that's true. It was actually an Indonesian program and a lot of the students came over from Indonesia with quite conservative Muslim attitudes, but it was just out there that Hugh and I were a couple. But we never actually pushed ourselves onto other people, or pushed any ideas onto them, so it was just accepted that we were a couple. Whatever they said in the background I don't know.

H: We do share quite a lot of common interests. We both like historic places, we both like nature, we also like comedy and magic. But we also deliberately spend some time each week doing things separately, because my firm belief is that if you don't do that, what else have you got to talk about? We also have slightly different friends connected with our different interests. I like going out to theatre and concerts a lot, Phillip not so much. Occasionally we do go as a couple, for instance we went to a concert together last night. Also we have joint bank accounts, we have joint ownership of the house, and, of course, we've protected each other with wills and powers of attorney. We did that very early in the relationship, but we also each have separate bank accounts and separate share portfolios.

P: So he's got money if he wants to buy something, and I've got money if I want to buy something as well, but we've also got money together when we want to buy things together. We've repeatedly told this to other gay couples and even suggested it a topic for a talk at the Uranians, but no one's been interested, as in how to manage money, how to manage financially.

H: It was a big issue for us after I lost my job with the ABC. Fortunately, Phillip's a very hard worker and he took on half the payment for the mortgage, so that was just incredibly helpful.

Hugh and Philip's Tips for Other Partners

P: (Tips for other couples) Have lots of sex I suppose, that's a good start.

H: Be prepared to compromise, know when to shut up, listen to each other a lot. If one of you wants to talk about something, put down your book or close the screen or whatever you're doing, and concentrate on what they say.

P: I suppose one of the big things is that you're in it together. That the neighbours aren't going to come along and help and make it all nice if it all goes pear-shaped. You're into it together and you've got to fix it.

H: And look for each other's good points, of course. Tell each other you love each other a lot.

Endnotes

Background information on LGBTIQ historical events

1: Clive Moore and Bryan Jamison, Vol. 14, No. 2, 2007 Queensland's Criminal Justice System and Homosexuality, 1860–1954.

2: *https://www.legislation.qld.gov.au/view/pdf/2014-08-29/act-1899-009*

3: Jo Lennan and George Williams, *The Death Penalty in Australian Law*, Sydney Law Review

4: https://www.sbs.com.au/topics/sexuality/feature/secret-history-australias-gay-diggers-anzac

5: https://books.google.com.au/books?hl=en&lr=&id=EvBMyR1hr2wC&oi=fnd&pg=PR9&dq=1960s+political+lgbt+movements&ots=YKMAR7Vowg&sig=hqowT_ypTyBBxFiK7vy6ArRDBrk#v=onepage&q=1960s%20political%20lgbt%20movements&f=false

6: http://www.theage.com.au/news/Reviews/Gay-old-time/2005/01/19/1106110804743.html

7: https://books.google.com.au/books?id=5SN ZKnyzYgYC&pg=PA7&lpg=PA7&dq=homose xuals+security+at+risk+ASIO&source=bl&ots =X1_PKb22UB&sig=wMJ4v_4xsS_ahIIi2Eg1dyNK UGE&hl=en&sa=X&ved=0ahUKEwjjh-aFjJzXA hUEE5QKHbHxDswQ6AEIQTAD#v=onepage &q=homosexuals%20security%20at%20risk%20 ASIO&f=false.

8: http://camp.org.au/component/content/article?id=138

9: http://www.abc.net.au/archives/80days/stories/2012/01/19/3411558.htm

10: Michael Kirby, The 1973 Deletion of Homosexuality as a Psychiatric Disorder: 30 Years on, First Published December 1, 2003

11: http://www.sbs.com.au/topics/sexuality/agenda/article/2016/08/12/definitive-timeline-lgbt-rights-australia

12: http://www.mardigras.org.au/history/

13: http://www.theaidsinstitute.org/node/259

14: http://www.theaidsinstitute.org/node/259

15: https://www.legislation.sa.gov.au/LZ/C/A/EQUAL%20OPPORTUNITY%20ACT%201984.aspx

16: https://www.humanrights.gov.au/publications/same-sex-same-entitlements-chapter-15

17: https://www.legislation.gov.au/Details/C2004A04852

18: http://www.utas.edu.au/library/companion_to_tasmanian_history/G/Gay%20Law%20Reform.htm

19: https://www.aph.gov.au/Parliamentary_Business/Bills_Legislation/bd/bd0405/05bd005

20: https://www.dss.gov.au/our-responsibilities/families-and-children/programs-services/recognition-of-same-sex-relationships

21: http://www.abc.net.au/news/2013-12-12/high-court-decision-on-act-same-sex-marriage-laws/5152168

22: http://www.sbs.com.au/topics/sexuality/agenda/article/2016/11/21/gay-adoption-set-be-legal-every-australian-state

23: http://www.heraldsun.com.au/news/victoria/abs-chief-statistician-david-kalisch-makes-nation-wait-for-ssm-answer/news-story/8b86ff758fe1991a834ef305fb50776f

www.ingramcontent.com/pod-product-compliance
Lightning Source LLC
Chambersburg PA
CBHW030434010526
44118CB00011B/637